THE POPE
AND THE PANDEMIC

*Lessons in Leadership
in a Time of Crisis*

AGBONKHIANMEGHE E. OROBATOR, SJ

ORBIS BOOKS
www.orbisbooks.com

ORBIS ⊕ BOOKS
Maryknoll, New York 10545

Fathers and Brothers
MARYKNOLL™

Founded in 1970, Orbis Books endeavors to publish works that enlighten the mind, nourish the spirit, and challenge the conscience. The publishing arm of the Maryknoll Fathers and Brothers, Orbis seeks to explore the global dimensions of the Christian faith and mission, to invite dialogue with diverse cultures and religious traditions, and to serve the cause of reconciliation and peace. The books published reflect the views of their authors and do not represent the official position of the Maryknoll Society. To learn more about Maryknoll and Orbis Books, please visit our website at www.maryknollsociety.org.

Library of Congress Cataloging-in-Publication Data

Names: Orobator, A. E., author.
Title: The Pope and the pandemic : lessons in leadership in a time of crisis / Agbonkhianmeghe E. Orobator, SJ.
Description: Maryknoll, NY : Orbis Books, [2021] | Includes bibliographical references and index. | Summary: "Through an examination of Pope Francis's words and actions during the coronavirus pandemic, the author finds a model of leadership for a suffering world"— Provided by publisher.
Identifiers: LCCN 2020040778 (print) | LCCN 2020040779 (ebook) | ISBN 9781626984189 (trade paperback) | ISBN 9781608338818 (epub)
Subjects: LCSH: Francis, Pope, 1936– | Leadership—Religious aspects—Catholic Church. | COVID-19 (Disease)
Classification: LCC BX1378.7 .O75 2021 (print) | LCC BX1378.7 (ebook) | DDC 262/.13—dc23
LC record available at https://lccn.loc.gov/2020040778
LC ebook record available at https://lccn.loc.gov/2020040779

*To all the precious lives lost and to the heroic
frontline and essential workers who have kept
humanity and hope alive in the midst of COVID-19.*

Contents

Acknowledgments

Were COVID-19 a thing of blessing I would have credited it with the inspiration to write this book. Although the idea of writing a book on Pope Francis's leadership predated the pandemic, this project only came to fruition during the long, bleak, and pernicious period of crisis unleashed by a virulent plague. Propitiously, writing it proved to be a mitigating factor in dealing with the consequent involuntary confinement. Full credit must of course go to the main character, Pope Francis. I have no doubt that the world urgently needs a few good women and men to model what good leadership looks like, especially in a time of crisis. Francis is one such person. My intention in this book is not to flatter, idolize, or canonize him, as if he needed anybody's favor to burnish his image as a global icon, brand, and leader. This book fulfills a debt of gratitude to him as a personal quest to learn from one of the greats of church and human history in whose times I feel privileged and grateful to be living.

I presented this project to Orbis Books as I was nearing the completion of the first draft. Amazingly, publisher and editor in chief Robert Ellsberg offered me a contract in record time. His enthusiastic reception of my manuscript confirmed the timeliness and relevance of this book for understanding the unique leadership role of Pope Francis in global affairs and for learning how to envisage and strive for the advent of an alternative world in conformity with God's dream. I am profoundly grateful to Robert and his excellent team at Orbis, in particular Dr. Jill Brennan O'Brien, who diligently and meticulously shepherded this book through editorial preparation to publication.

My Jesuit community of John the Baptist Anyeh-Zamcho, Paul Hamill, Elphège Quenum, Charles Chilufya, and Fernando Saldivar created a genial ambience of fraternal companionship that greatly aided me in writing this book.

As always, my final word of gratitude goes to my soulmate from God, Oghomwen n'Oghomwen Dr. Anne Arabome, SSS, who first conceived of the idea to write a book about Pope Francis; my brother, Chuks Afiawari, SJ; and Kijana wa Zamani Joe Healey, MM.

Asanteni sana!

Abbreviations

CA   *Centisimus annus* (The Hundredth Year). Pope John Paul II, encyclical, May 1, 1991

CST   Catholic social teaching (also catholic social thinking; catholic social thought)

EG   *Evangelii gaudium* (The Joy of the Gospel). Pope Francis, apostolic exhortation on the church's mission of evangelization in the modern world, November 24, 2013

GE   *Gaudete et exsultate* (Rejoice and Be Glad). Pope Francis, apostolic exhortation on the universal call to holiness, March 19, 2018

LS   *Laudato si'* (Praise Be to You). Pope Francis, encyclical on care for our common home, May 24, 2015

MV   *Misericordiae vultus* (The Face of Mercy). Pope Francis, bull of indiction of the Extraordinary Jubilee of Mercy, April 11, 2015

PHEIC   Public Health Emergency of International Concern

RN   *Rerum novarum* (Of the New Things). Pope Leo XIII, social encyclical, May 15, 1891

Sp. Ex. *Spiritual Exercises of St. Ignatius of Loyola*

SRS   *Sollicitudo rei socialis* (On Social Concern). Pope John Paul II, encyclical, December 30, 1987

UK	United Kingdom
UN	United Nations
US	United States of America
WHO	World Health Organization

Introduction

We Don't Need Another Hero

We are witnesses to these things.

—Acts 5:32

In 2020, a crisis of unprecedented proportion erupted, roiled, and changed the world abruptly, unexpectedly, and irreversibly. By nature, a crisis is a complex occurrence or situation that reveals a range of associated multilayered conditions of societal dysfunctionalities. At first glance, such an occurrence may seem to be a simple fact or outcome of social existence. It can, however, very quickly evolve into an enormous challenge, generate a complex set of problems, and exacerbate existing and precarious societal conditions.[1] Regardless of how it manifests, a crisis poses a grave threat to existing arrangements at personal and collective levels of existence.

---

[1] This idea is analogous to what English anthropologist Timothy Jenkins describes as an "algebra of implication" or a "can of worms." In the local English society that he studies, he discovers that the kin relationship and acquaintances among local families are so complex that it is practically impossible to deal with an individual without implicating the extensive range of the person's familial relationships. Timothy Jenkins, *Religion in English Everyday Life: An Ethnographic Approach* (New York: Berghahn Books, 1999), 109–37.

This understanding of crisis aptly defines the coronavirus disease of 2019 (COVID-19) that has rattled the entire global population in unparalleled ways as a contagious virus of frightening potential and scale, inflicting incalculable damage on lives and livelihoods. The ravaging march of this virus brought the world to a standstill or, more accurately, to its knees. Everything either stopped or closed, and almost overnight a new vocabulary of lockdown and isolation gained prominence. The surviving global population counts as living witnesses to an apocalyptic occurrence that cut swaths of bodily and economic destruction and sowed mayhem across the world. There is a growing collection of narratives that attempt to understand the multifaceted dimensions and consequences of the crisis engendered by the coronavirus pandemic. Aside from the human cost, as yet to be fully computed in personal, social, and economic terms, the tragedy of COVID-19 also surfaces questions for deeper reflection, study, and understanding. The specific purpose of this book, which explores and examines the leadership dimensions of the crisis, is to study and reflect on Pope Francis's leadership during a global health emergency that has paralyzed the world.

A disclaimer is in order here. I am an admirer of Pope Francis and, like him, I am a Jesuit. My vocational identity does not account for my admiration for the pope, however. The idea of writing a book on leadership predates COVID-19, but this crisis turned out to be a somewhat auspicious context and moment for its actualization. Francis's approach to the crisis exemplifies a certain style of leadership that is worth paying attention to, particularly as part of a process of learning the lessons of the coronavirus crisis.[2] Leadership is critical in times

---

[2] In speaking of "lessons," I do not imply that the coronavirus pandemic is an occurrence with some implicit or explicit meaning, be it instructive or punitive, naturally or supernaturally instigated. I thus apply the notion of *kairos* with caution. The role of pandemics in the social construction of reality from a religious perspective is a contested subject

of uncertainty, and the coronavirus pandemic has exposed a deep crisis in leadership on a global scale. This public health emergency has subjected the notion and practice of leadership to a stress test, and judging by the performance of leaders across the globe, the report card has revealed significant gaps, mistakes, and failures. From Brazil to Britain, the US to India, and all across the continents of Europe, Asia, Latin America, Oceania, and Africa, heroes and heroines have emerged from the debris of this crisis. Conversely, there is no dearth of villains and charlatans masquerading as leaders, all the while lacking empathy, honesty, and aptitude. When their prevarications and procrastinations are exposed, some of these straw men (they are almost exclusively men!) have downplayed the severity of the viral outbreak as a hoax, or as an illness no worse than the seasonal flu or even the sniffles. Others have resorted to a crude blame game, even as infections and deaths from COVID-19 rose alarmingly. Some names inevitably come to mind, but I abstain from listing them. Those who are in the group of heroes and heroines have been justly recognized and feted for handling the crisis with foresight, resolve, empathy, and integrity. In particular, their focus rested solidly on advancing the causes of solidarity, human dignity, and the common good. Their concern for human life rightly took precedence over short-term political considerations. In contrast, the impostors fell short on all counts, blundering their way through a life-threatening global health crisis and squandering the opportunity to contain an outbreak the scale of which is unprecedented in the modern era. This book offers a critique of such leadership gaps simply by highlighting Francis's leadership style and preferences. While some politicians have seen their credibility collapse due to their inept management of the coronavirus pandemic, I believe that Francis has stood out as a global reference point. This book is

---

among historians, sociologists, and theologians. See Stephen Bullivant, *Catholicism in the Time of Coronavirus* (Park Ridge, IL: Word on Fire, 2020), 1–9, www.wordonfire.org.

a reflection on how one person leads by word and by deed in extraordinary and challenging times, and on what lessons we can draw from his example.

Of course, Pope Francis is not an elected political leader. He lives in a ninety-one-year-old UNESCO-designated World Heritage site, variously named "Holy See," "Vatican City," or "the Vatican," which has fewer than a thousand citizens. Amid the coronavirus crisis, he was not saddled with the burden of making consequential decisions, like how to run a national health service, when to impose or ease a lockdown, or how to safely reopen and revive a battered or collapsed national economy. But he exercises authority beyond the walls of the Vatican over Catholicism's global community of approximately 1.3 billion adherents, and his influence as a leader often intersects with political and economic domains. He famously elevated politics to a quasi-religious dais when he declared it one of the highest forms of charity. Since his election to the papacy in 2013, he has demonstrated a kind of prophetic and pastoral leadership that seeks to be inclusive yet decisive in reforming the politics, economics, and practices of the Roman Catholic Church. His style prioritizes the communicative ethics of *parrhesia*, that is, the ability to speak with boldness and listen with humility. Even outside of the church, his leadership and authoritative voice continue to reverberate across a global landscape, encompassing topical issues such as ecology, economics, armed conflict, international migration, and nationalism.

Since the election of Pope Francis, many columnists and scholars, commentators and pundits, Vaticanologists and journalists seem to have happened upon a new, prolific, and, perhaps, lucrative enterprise of decoding, deconstructing, and deciphering the 266th successor to Peter. Their mixed motives have produced mixed results. In the assessment of one expert, Francis "is a complex man, not easily analyzed."[3] Notwith-

---

[3] John O'Malley, "Reconciling Doctrine, Theology, Spirituality, and Pastorality," in *Pope Francis: A Voice for Mercy, Justice, Love, and Care*

standing, there is no shortage of books on Francis the pope, leader, reformer, teacher, advocate, and Jesuit.[4] Each of these books offers fascinating and valuable insights into Francis's dynamic personality, profound wisdom, and revolutionary vision for church and society, all of which have served him well as a leader—occasionally, however, he has drawn the ire of detractors and adversaries, and even inspired a few counter-narratives.[5] This book departs from the trajectory and emphases of current studies of Pope Francis, and focuses solely on the art of leading in a time of crisis. The specific but universal context for undertaking this study is the coronavirus pandemic. The principal premise is that Francis's leadership has not been confined to his Catholic flock; its reach has extended across the globe. By reflecting upon his words and deeds, I pay close attention to how the pope's handling of the crisis exemplifies a certain style of leadership that in turn reflects his overall pastoral and prophetic style of ministry. As such, I believe that the lessons identified and examined in this book will be valuable for a global audience of people in leadership positions, both in the church and in the broader society.

---

for the Earth, ed. Barbara E. Wall and Massimo Faggioli (Maryknoll, NY: Orbis Books, 2019), 21.

[4] The list includes the following recent releases: Austen Ivereigh, *Wounded Shepherd: Pope Francis's Struggle to Convert the Catholic Church* (New York: Henry Holt, 2019); Massimo Faggioli, *The Liminal Papacy of Pope Francis: Moving toward Global Catholicity* (Maryknoll, NY: Orbis Books, 2020); Christopher Lamb, *The Outsider: Pope Francis and His Battle to Reform the Church* (Maryknoll, NY: Orbis Books, 2020); Gerard O'Connell, *The Election of Pope Francis: An Inside Account of the Conclave That Changed History* (Maryknoll, NY: Orbis Books, 2019); and Barbara E. Wall and Massimo Faggioli, eds., *Pope Francis: A Voice for Mercy, Justice, Love, and Care for the Earth* (Maryknoll, NY: Orbis Books, 2019).

[5] For example, H. J. A. Sire (aka Marcantonio Colonna), *The Dictator Pope: The Inside Story of the Francis Papacy* (Washington, DC: Regnery Publishing, 2017).

New York on My Mind

In the afternoon of Tuesday, April 14, 2020, the Archbishop of New York Archdiocese, Cardinal Timothy Dolan, answered a telephone call from the Vatican. The caller was Pope Francis. Under normal circumstances such a call would have been routine and not newsworthy. But the context was significant: New York State had become the epicenter of the coronavirus pandemic in the US. Outside of Italy and Spain, the state was recording the largest daily rates of infection, and it had more coronavirus fatalities than any other state in the country. New York was on the mind of Francis when he called Cardinal Dolan to—according to the latter's social media account— "express his love, concern, and closeness to all the people of New York, especially those who are sick, during the coronavirus outbreak." "New Yorkers," said the pope, "are in my prayers in a special way at this time." As mentioned, ordinarily, there wouldn't be anything particularly remarkable about a midafternoon international call from one religious leader to another. But from the perspective of this book, the papal phone call spoke volumes. The cardinal's response to Francis helps to elucidate the focus and rationale of this book: "I thanked the Pope for *the leadership he has displayed during this global pandemic*, and assured him of the love and prayers of the people of New York for him and his ministry."[6] A crisis can illuminate the exercise or practice of (good) leadership. However, the kind of leadership displayed by Francis was not always in evidence, even among religious leaders.

This book is about a global icon and his leadership style in the midst of a global crisis. It is neither a character study nor a biopic; it is also not simply a historical account of how Pope Francis handled the coronavirus crisis, though a sequence of

---

[6] Robin Gomes, "Covid-19: Pope Calls to Express His Closeness to New Yorkers," *Vatican News*, April 15, 2020 (www.vaticannews.va). Emphasis mine.

events will be recounted to set the context for the discussion. Some of the previously mentioned books have dealt almost exhaustively with the character and biography of Francis. The methodology adopted for this book is best described as a complementary dual approach: (1) it observes and examines the activities of the pope during the coronavirus crisis, asking how Pope Francis has led in such challenging times and circumstances; (2) it distills the constitutive elements of leadership in the particular moment of the coronavirus crisis, asking and attempting to answer the questions: What does good leadership look like during a crisis? What does Francis's leadership teach us in a time of crisis?

In the ongoing quest to discover and learn the lessons of the coronavirus pandemic for all facets of life, it is critically important to identify, analyze, and draw leadership lessons for the future of the world, whether or not the virus is eradicated. To my knowledge, there is as yet no such study that profiles the leadership of Pope Francis in the context of the coronavirus crisis.[7] There is a relatively small body of literature on leadership in times of crisis that focuses on the coronavirus pandemic, but these works deal almost exclusively with corporate and country leadership.[8] As a result, but understandably, such literature overlooks people like Francis. In exploring these questions, I do not intend to enter into dialogue or

---

[7] Antonio Spadaro's article, "Pope Francis and the Coronavirus Crisis," in *La Civiltà Cattolica*, April 9, 2020 (www.laciviltacattolica.com), reflects on and highlights the key points of Pope Francis's interview with Austen Ivereigh, "Take Care of Yourselves for a Future That Will Come," *The Tablet* (April 11, 2020).

[8] See, for example, Michaela J. Kerrissey and Amy C. Edmondson, "What Good Leadership Looks Like during This Pandemic," *Harvard Business Review*, April 13, 2020 (www.hbr.org); Gemma D'Auria and Aaron De Smet, "Leadership in a Crisis: Responding to the Coronavirus Outbreak and Future Challenges," *McKinsey & Company*, March 16, 2020 (www.mckinsey.com).

dispute with theoretical and conceptual models of leadership. My aims and purposes are modest: I am asking, "What do we need to learn from the way that Francis has gone about fulfilling his duties as a leader in the heat of a global public health crisis?" Not every leader will have to face a crisis of the same magnitude as the coronavirus pandemic. But a crisis is a crisis no matter the level at which it occurs. In the wider context of leadership, the dynamics of a crisis are clearly distinguishable: it tests our resolve, shakes our confidence, and challenges our convictions. There is a slight chance that by the time this book is published the world will have moved on—but, in all likelihood, a global reckoning may still be in progress. The heroes and heroines will continue to be recognized and feted, while the villains and charlatans will be unmasked and castigated.

The sources used for this book include the homilies, reflections, messages, statements, and prayers of Pope Francis. The contexts and circumstances of their delivery are varied; they include the scheduled weekly Angelus address, Regina Caeli address, and papal audiences, as well as the specially arranged liturgical events at the Vatican, including the pope's daily Eucharistic celebrations in the chapel of Casa Santa Marta. The pope is a global public figure who is never far from the scrutinizing eyes of journalists, correspondents, and reporters, both accredited and freelancers. I had the privilege of accessing numerous sources of rich information on the pope's daily activities during the pandemic in religious and secular newspapers, magazines, agencies, online news feeds, and journals, most of them marked by excellent journalism and reporting. Although the pope comes across as reserved and self-effacing, there are important interviews conducted by seasoned journalists that open a window into his thinking and offer insights on his approach to leadership in a time of crisis. The main character of this book is not a passive object of study lending itself to a narrow analysis; the consideration of the materials on Pope Francis in a time of crisis entails a process of evaluation, interpretation, and judgment from which emerge the main lessons set forth in this book. Some readers could conceivably and rightly draw alternative and less flattering conclusions about the pope and his leadership of the church, either in a time of crisis or in general.

Besides the pope's words, of greater significance are his actions, decisions, and gestures in the midst of the coronavirus pandemic. If actions speak louder than words, Francis is a master of the power of symbolism. I have dedicated chapters 1 and 4 to the potency and authenticity of gestures that transcend mere rhetoric. Also, in these chapters, I explore the use and efficacy of symbolism, spoken and enacted, as a medium of messaging in a time of crisis. What is clear is that the combination of sources—Francis's words and deeds—constitutes a powerful message of faith, hope, love, care, solidarity, and compassion in a time of crisis. The peak of this compendium of messaging falls within Lent and Eastertide of 2020. Together these two high liturgical seasons of the church provide a salubrious backdrop for confronting the headwinds of despair, fear, and death occasioned by the coronavirus pandemic. Through a close study of Pope Francis's statements and actions during these moments it is possible to trace the contours of his leadership, one that inspires and instructs, consoles and comforts, especially in challenging times.

Keep in Mind

To understand the thrust of the analysis and reflections contained in this book, it is important to keep five considerations in mind. First, the documentary materials and empirical evidence collected and examined for this book have a fixed timeline. Chinese officials first reported the existence of atypical cases of pneumonia in Wuhan, China, to the World Health Organization's (WHO) China Country Office in Beijing on December 31, 2019. A month later, on January 30, 2020, the

WHO declared the outbreak a Public Health Emergency of International Concern. The coronavirus quickly spread across the world along a frightening trajectory that has left no country untouched. By July 2020, most countries had begun the complicated process of easing or lifting restrictions on social encounter, commercial activities, educational institutions, and human mobility, though strict prevention guidelines were introduced to stave off a second wave of infection. Despite continuing spikes and outbreaks, people across the world had become weary of lockdown, even as the WHO warned nations about the threat of a new and dangerous phase of the coronavirus pandemic.

This timeline of my writing is thus approximately six months, from December 2019 to July 2020. In one sense, this is a short time in which to make the kind of argument attempted in this book.[9] It is reassuring, though, that some of the lessons in leadership presented here have been verified and attested to by other writers and authors who have studied Pope Francis's handling of other crises and how he exemplifies a certain style of leadership. It could be argued that these lessons do not tell us much that is new about the leadership abilities of Francis; nonetheless, there is an added value in accentuating new and unique facets of those abilities in the exceptional circumstances of the coronavirus crisis. As will become evident in the chapters of this book, the discussion occasionally widens to address significant aspects of Francis's theological outlook and ethical preferences. These forays are neither fortuitous nor futile; the book aims to provide a wider context and framework for situating, interpreting, and understanding the distinctiveness of the pope's approach to leadership within his overall pastoral and prophetic style of ministry.

---

[9] Mine is a generous timespan compared to Bullivant's *Catholicism in the Time of Coronavirus,* written "over the space of twelve days: Monday, March 30, to Friday, April 10, 2020," vii.

Second, I mentioned that Pope Francis is not a leader in the manner of contemporary political leaders. He leads a global community of believers who adhere to a set of beliefs, practice prescribed rituals, and undertake actions that embody their faith convictions. Yet the political implications of Francis's words and deeds are as influential and far-reaching as his audience is global and diverse. Amid the trials and tribulations of the pandemic, the pope has constructed and tailored his message to the world. Some readers may be familiar with the customary twice-yearly solemn blessing and message of popes for the city of Rome and for the entire world (his *Urbi et Orbi* address). While events such as this may be customary, by paying close attention to Pope Francis's performance, one notices that his approach to these functions is anything but the habitual indulgence of a custom. Whether he is conducting a solitary ritual in the cavernous St. Peter's Basilica or delivering a reflection in the Library of the Apostolic Palace at the Vatican, Francis occupies a global podium from which he addresses people worldwide. Every activity thus bears leadership implications. In chapter 5, I describe how the art and skill of bridging political, sectarian, and ideological divides rests on an extraordinary power to convene, in order to mobilize attention and action by people across the globe—an essential leadership quality in a time of crisis.

Third, although Pope Francis stands on and speaks from a global platform to a worldwide audience, he neither abuses the privilege nor plays to the gallery. Where some political leaders seemed to glory in the opportunity presented by the coronavirus crisis to track and improve their favorability ratings, Francis's intent was just the opposite. I cannot find any evidence to suggest that the pope either craved or courted the favorable opinion of his audience during the pandemic. Granted, he is not a political or partisan leader like the rest—but the gulf between the leadership style of Pope Francis and many world leaders represents a salient testimony to the importance of authentic leadership in a time of crisis. One poignant example may illustrate this point.

In a gesture reminiscent of the practice of some political leaders, Francis made a surprise call-in to a live Italian TV show on Good Friday 2020. The host—Lorena Bianchetti of *A Sua Immagine* (In His Image) on Italy's Rai 1 channel—was visibly startled by the unexpected papal call. People who are familiar with the media circus orchestrated by certain politicians may find the tone and content of the pope's TV conversation unusual at first. Of particular significance was the fact that the pope did not call in to dispute an ideological point, excoriate an irritating anchor, or pitch a political agenda. In a soothing and calming voice, Pope Francis shared his thought and preoccupation during the coronavirus pandemic with the program's audience. In the context of a liturgical season commemorating the suffering and death of Jesus of Nazareth, Francis revealed that foremost in his thought were the "many crucified people in history and those of today." They included, said the pope, the frontline health care workers in this pandemic, people "who die for love" and for the victims of COVID-19. Pope Francis professed his closeness to all those offering their lives to help others: "I am close to the people of God . . . close to the pain of the world. I am close, I am close to you all." The call lasted a few brief minutes, but it moved the show's host to tears.

There are many lessons to be learned from this brief and seemingly insignificant TV moment from the perspective of leadership. These lessons are outlined in three chapters of this book: in chapter 1, I discuss the paramount importance of providing a consoling accompaniment embodied in poignant gestures and symbols that communicate compassion, mercy, and hope in a time of crisis; in chapter 2, I focus on the significance of a preferential love for the poor, marginalized, and vulnerable people who bear the brunt of crises such as a pandemic; and in chapter 3, I consider the importance of celebrating the goodness of humanity that shines through in the generosity and sacrifice of frontline workers. Taken together, my point is that these three elements illustrate essential qualities of leadership in a time of crisis.

There is a minor but important addendum to the preceding point. It concerns the fact that COVID-19 hit the world around the time of the seventh anniversary of the pontificate of Pope Francis. Although not given to a life of ostentation and ceremony, there wasn't a hint that Francis considered March 13, 2020, an important milestone to be marked at the height of a global crisis. The extraordinary circumstances created by the coronavirus pandemic completely eclipsed any thought of a papal celebration. I recall receiving an invitation from the Apostolic Nunciature in Nairobi, Kenya, in early February 2020, to a cocktail reception to mark the anniversary of Francis's election as pope. A few weeks later, the event was cancelled on account of the coronavirus pandemic. As the pope indicated to Lorena Bianchetti and her live TV audience, empathy, compassion, and closeness to the pain and anguish of the people were his unalloyed concerns in the time of the coronavirus crisis. As I point out in this book, the ability to focus on things that matter represents a key component of leadership in a time of crisis. Human dignity and the common good trump narrow and selfish interests.

Fourth, during the coronavirus pandemic, the use of authority mattered. Governments scrambled a raft of measures to contain, mitigate, and combat the virus: lockdowns, curfews, confinement, isolation, quarantines, stay-at-home and shelter-in-place orders, restrictions on mobility, and social distancing. As images online and on cable TV showed, in some places, these measures were enforced with brute force. Leader after leader spoke forcefully about the pandemic using military language, as if waging a war against a ruthless and invisible assailant. Across the world, some presidents and heads of governments seized the opportunity to revel in the practice of prefacing and qualifying their title with the adjective "war-time." Whether they understood this nomenclature literally or metaphorically, at times it came at a deadly cost. At one point in Nigeria, for example, more people had been killed by security operatives ostensibly enforcing lockdown and curfew than had succumbed to the coronavirus. According to data collected by the National Human Rights Commission and the Ministry of Health, barely two weeks into a partial lockdown in Nigeria, law enforcers had killed eighteen people, compared with twelve who had died from the coronavirus. Other law enforcers reportedly raped and assaulted women in Rwanda and Uganda, and Indian security forces moved against tens of thousands of migrant laborers who were demanding to return to their rural areas to increase their chances of surviving the effects of a nationwide lockdown. Where curfews were imposed, as in Nigeria, Uganda, and Kenya, there were reports of unlawful detention or abuse of people who were breaking curfew because they were desperately searching for food. Some Kenyan police infamously resorted to extorting bribes from curfew offenders by threatening to remand them in quarantine centers for up to twenty-eight days. In the US, racial prejudice claimed collateral victims through racial profiling and police brutality.[10]

Such instances reveal how the abuse of authority—such as by resorting to excessive force during a crisis like a pandemic—risks confusing the threat (a virus) with the victims (people). This book offers a critique of leadership that is predicated on coercion and the use of force. With the help of

---

[10] See Malaika Jabali, "Coronavirus Policing Leads to Harsher Repercussions for Black Americans," *The Guardian*, April 15, 2020 (www.theguardian.com); Sheryl Gay Stolberg, "'Pandemic within a Pandemic': Coronavirus and Police Brutality Roil Black Communities," *New York Times*, June 7, 2020 (www.nytimes.com); and Rashid Shabazz, "We Can't Breathe: COVID-19 and Police Injustice Are Suffocating Black People," *The Root*, May 29, 2020 (www.theroot.com).

many examples, I will illustrate how Pope Francis prioritizes the needs of vulnerable people and how he repeatedly invites wielders of authority to exercise their political vocation as a service to solidarity, the common good, and the advancement of human dignity during and after the pandemic.

It should be said that not all regimes have been authoritarian and brutal during this time. There are several instances in which authority is exercised with caution and consideration, reminding people of the need to protect others by protecting themselves. The standard public health advice advocates almost altruistically caring for the well-being of others and thinking less of self without any added external compulsion to abide by this advice. The use of violence to enforce containment measures contrasts drastically with the strategy of appealing to moral authority. Pope Francis's style epitomizes the latter approach. There isn't the slightest hint in his messaging about coercive measures or the violent enforcement of civic restrictions on people and their physical movements. Chapter 5 also examines the moral authority of a leader as a critical asset for initiating constructive engagement across political and partisan divides in a time of crisis. Beyond engaging other leaders, to be effective, the exercise of moral authority during a crisis must raise awareness and draw attention to the values and priorities that uphold human life and rights rather than undermine them.

Fifth, the coronavirus pandemic has affected all segments of the global community without exception, including faith communities. In particular, it has generated unforeseen and unprecedented circumstances, challenges, and changes in the way Christians experience the church as a local and global community of believers. Places of worship were shuttered across the world, denying millions of adherents the opportunity to physically participate in worship celebration for an indeterminate period. Interestingly, the curtailing of sacramental and congregational worship spurred believers to discover unorthodox spaces for communion and connection. Many have invented creative and alternative ways of celebrating and ministering using relatively affordable online tools; yet, the sudden loss of a physical community also has irked and frustrated many worshippers waiting impatiently for the COVID-19 storm to pass. The point here is that the crisis signaled a crisis for all traditions of faith. Who can forget the incredible images of a white-clad Pope Francis shuffling across the vast empty square of Saint Peter's or gazing over a deserted square from the window of the Apostolic Palace to impart a blessing (virtually) on the city and the world? These unparalleled scenes evidence the changes foisted on religious communities across the world by the pandemic. More crucially, the global public health catastrophe has raised pertinent questions within religious communities about how to lead in a time of crisis, particularly the necessity of change, flexibility, and adaptability to the circumstances and challenges forced upon them by the pandemic. Managing change, demonstrating flexibility, and adapting to a fast-moving crisis are important components of effective leadership in a time of crisis. This will be the subject of chapter 6.

Not Yet Easter

One final admission. This book is in part the outcome of a personal quest for light in the nebulous fog of a crisis. The regnant view seems to present the coronavirus crisis as a purely epidemiological event with social, economic, and political consequences. That is to say, "The coronavirus pandemic puts societies to the test: it is a test of political leadership, of national health systems, of social care services, of solidarity, of the social contract—a test of our very own fabric."[11] This

---

[11] Editorial, "COVID-19 Puts Societies to the Test," *The Lancet 5* no. 5 (May 1, 2020): E235, www.thelancet.com. Slovenian philosopher Slavoj Žižek sees the coronavirus pandemic as a triple crisis, namely, medical, economic, and psychological, in *Pandemic! COVID-19 Shakes*

view is partial and incomplete. In the perspective of this book, the coronavirus pandemic is also a test of faith. On a personal level, I believe that I am not alone in admitting to the fact that the coronavirus pandemic has tested the conviction of my faith, shaken the foundation of my hope, and challenged the basis of my actions as a Christian and a global citizen.

In a special moment of prayer on March 27, 2020, Pope Francis called the pandemic a "thick darkness" that "has gathered over our squares, our streets, and our cities; it has taken over our lives, filling everything with a deafening silence and a distressing void, that stops everything as it passes by; we feel it in the air, we notice in people's gestures, their glances give them away."[12] It was an apt assessment. Although Easter 2020 fell in the heat of the pandemic, I defiantly resolved to remain in the dark passion of the times. I felt this resolution was justifiable because as long as the cloud of COVID-19 cast a macabre shadow over hope and blighted human lives, it was not yet Easter. Until God had banished the specter of death by coronavirus, I could not sing the *Exsultet*, the traditional hymn of the resurrected Lord, with confidence and joy. Only when I began to pay close attention to the words and actions of Pope Francis in the gloom of the crisis did I begin to perceive a flicker of light and a glimmer of hope. That is why I am convinced that Francis exemplifies what good leadership looks like in a time of crisis.

Like me, people across the globe were caught amid the chaos provoked by the fear of a deadly and invisible enemy. This chaos was compounded by a cacophony of messages about the nature of the disease, a plethora of fake news promoting dubious remedies, apprehension about serious economic havoc, and the lack of a robust health care strategy. But perhaps the most influential negative factor in the current

---

the World (New York: Polity Press, 2020).

[12] "Extraordinary Moment of Prayer Presided Over by Pope Francis," Friday, March 27, 2020 (www.vatican.va).

situation is the irrational, fickle, and inept leadership displayed in some parts of the world, which has led to mass discontent as citizens lose confidence in the willingness and ability of their leaders to guide them out of disaster. Francis, in contrast to some recognizably incompetent, selfish, and egotistic politicians and partisans, proffered a breath of fresh air much in character with his preferred model of prophetic and pastoral leadership. Yet he would be loath to cast himself as a hero of the coronavirus crisis. Predictably, as I show in this book, he reserves this accolade for others. A few months into his pontificate, when Italian Jesuit priest and journalist Antonio Spadaro offered Pope Francis an opportunity to toot his own horn, he retorted with a frank and disarming admission: "I am a sinner whom the Lord has looked upon." Now in his seventh year as pope, it would seem that His Holiness has made only modest progress, judging by his admission to another journalist, Austen Ivereigh, author of *Wounded Shepherd: Pope Francis's Struggle to Convert the Catholic Church*: "Of course I have my areas of selfishness. On Tuesdays, my confessor comes, and I take care of things there."[13] An honest self-awareness is an established factor of credible leadership, as I will underscore in chapter 6.

In this book, I argue that the manner in which people, communities, and societies around the world respond and adapt to a crisis depends to a considerable extent on the caliber and quality of leadership available to them. Courageous, competent, committed, conscientious, and compassionate leadership is an asset for navigating the uncertainty of crisis in order to protect and save lives. When leaders live up to their solemn responsibilities and commitments, they can be the difference between light and darkness, hope and despair, life and death for the people whom they have the privilege of serving and protecting. In the final analysis, true leadership is forged in the vicarious crucible of crisis. This in sum is the thesis of this book.

---

[13] Ivereigh, "Take Care of Yourselves for a Future That Will Come," 6.

I

Office of Consolation

Console, O console my people, says your God.

—*Isaiah 40:1*

St. Ignatius of Loyola (1491–1556), founder of the Society of Jesus (Jesuits), is recognized as one of the most influential figures in the Roman Catholic Counter-Reformation in the sixteenth century. His greatest legacy, though, is his contribution to the development of Christian spirituality through his *Spiritual Exercises*. Briefly, the *Spiritual Exercises* is a user manual and guide containing meditative and contemplative practices (retreats) spread over four weeks and adapted to the needs and circumstances of the user. Drawing from gospel accounts, the manual meticulously follows the principal events of the life, ministry, death, and resurrection of Jesus Christ.

In the fourth week of the *Spiritual Exercises* (*Sp. Ex.*), Ignatius imaginatively describes the newly resurrected Jesus as appearing first to his mother, Mary: "After Christ died on the cross, his body remained separated from his soul but always united with his divinity. . . . and rising again, he appeared in body and soul to his Blessed Mother" (*Sp. Ex.*, 219). Ignatius is not oblivious to the possibility of controversy arising from this apocryphal vignette. After all, this was the high tide of the

Inquisition. But viewed from the wider context of Christ's crucifixion, his approach would make eminent sense—no doubt
Mary's emotional trauma was still intense over the weekend
of the torture and brutal killing of her son, as were the sorrow and pain of her fellow disciples, in particular Mary Magdalene. Pope Francis espouses a similar understanding in his
Easter Vigil 2020 homily, by stating that "Our Lady spent that
Saturday, the day that would be dedicated to her, in prayer
and hope. She responded to sorrow with trust in the Lord."
The combination of Ignatius's version and Francis's reflection leads to one probable outcome: Mary's prayer and hope
would be rewarded with an unexpected visit by the resurrected
Lord. Transposed to a contemporary context, Mary's bereave-
ment would not have been unlike that of many families who
have lost loved ones to COVID-19, except for one emotionally wrenching difference. For the latter, participation in burial
rituals was either severely curtailed or practically impossible,
even for a spouse or children of the deceased. In the scenario
of Christ's dawn visit to his grieving mother, Ignatius invites
the retreatant to "Consider the office of consoler which Christ
our Lord carries out, and compare it with the way friends
console one another" (*Sp. Ex.*, 224). By the sheer brilliance of
his imagination, Ignatius reveals that the principal mission of
the resurrected Lord is as a purveyor of consolation. The Risen
Christ is the minister of consolation par excellence. The office
or ministry of consolation defines a constitutive dimension of
leadership in a time of crisis, and Pope Francis exemplifies this
dimension. A word on the notion of consolation in the spirituality of St. Ignatius is now in order.

In the *Spiritual Exercises*, Ignatius defines consolation simply as including "every increase in hope, faith, and love" (*Sp.
Ex.*, 316). The operative term is "increase." But the triple com-
position of consolation as a personal and collective experience
of hope, faith, and love is significant. For believers and nonbe-
lievers alike, these three elements constitute the first casualty

of the searing experience of a crisis like the coronavirus pandemic. As this rogue virus prowled the face of the earth, causing suffering and death, sowing fear and agony, and paralyzing the lives and livelihoods of millions of vulnerable women and men, inevitably questions about faith and hope have emerged with an increasing intensity: Where is God in all this? Does God care? It was as though, for many people, believing or not, the coronavirus crisis presented a fundamental test of faith. I recall that as people wrestled with this question, the editor of an Italian magazine dispatched an urgent note to me:

> We are living a very hard situation in Italy. We would like to give hope to our people and we are going to prepare a theological focus on Christian hope in this time. I am asking you one specific article about God and his presence during this time of coronavirus. "Where is God?" is a terrible question coming from the heart of many people.

Italy was at the time the epicenter of the pandemic in Europe. Amid the chaos and confusion of the global public health crisis, the image of an officer or minister of consolation fittingly describes a critical function of the leadership exemplified by Pope Francis.

Before setting out the factors that help illustrate the components of this leadership style, however, we must note a prior consideration. The exercise of this office of consolation abhors the temptation to sweeten or falsify the severity and pain of the pandemic or any similar crisis. As is typical of pandemics, COVID-19 caused and intensified the suffering of people across the world, leaving in its wake an incalculable toll of illness and death. The people who are not directly infected also experience suffering related to the virus, including mental health issues, like stress, anxiety, and depression; crisis-induced financial losses; and calamitous socioeconomic consequences. The mitigation of the multiple forms of suffering provoked by the coronavirus crisis formed part of the strategic responses of governments, humanitarian organizations, and business enterprises. Society's leaders also faced pressure to maintain a positive disposition or outlook. During pandemics, good news is a rare and highly prized currency. As COVID-19 sickened people and ravaged economies across the globe, one understandable instinct was an eagerness to devise or discover a quick and effective antidote such as a drug or vaccine. A tendency to craft slogans that proclaim the advent of better times, whether imagined or real, characterized the rhetoric of some politicians and partisans, with the result that some of them undermined the severity of the pandemic and precipitously announced a vision of light at the end of the tunnel or made false declarations of victory over the virus. This response is reminiscent of ancient biblical prophets who were derided for disguising their nostrums and platitudes as divine oracles, while recounting reckless lies and prophesying deceitful fantasies (see Jer 23:9–40). Furthermore, this approach is diametrically opposed to Jesus's way of consoling people in distress. In his homily in the chapel at Casa Santa Marta on May 8, 2020, Pope Francis identifies and elaborates "the three marks" of Christ in his role of consoler. First, the consolation of Christ is true, not deceiving. It is a consolation in closeness and silence, devoid of empty words. Second, it is not anesthesia. It neither signals nor offers a false comfort calculated to camouflage or numb pain and suffering. Third, it opens the door of hope. The resurrected Lord does not dodge discomfort and distress; rather, Christ journeys with people through painful realities into God's promise of consolation and peace. This three-step pedagogy of consolation finds concrete application in Francis's ministry of consolation. When Pope Francis called in to a live TV program to express his solidarity with frontline health care workers during the pandemic,[1] he was quick to underscore

---

[1] On Good Friday 2020, Francis called in and spoke to host Lorena Bianchetti of *A Sua Immagine* (In His Image) on Italy's Rai 1 channel.

the point that there was no quick fix or "happy ending" to the reality of the passion, suffering, and death of Jesus. As Francis explained, "Easter always ends in the Resurrection and in peace." However, this does not mean a "happy ending but a loving commitment that makes you tread a difficult path. But He trod it first. This comforts us and gives us strength." This ability to maintain a clear-headed and realistic outlook in the face of an overwhelming catastrophe and to refrain from indulging in false assurances represents an authenticity of purpose that is a key ingredient of leadership in a time of crisis.

A New Way of Being Close

On March 18, 2020, Pope Francis gave an exclusive interview to Paolo Rodari, the Vatican correspondent of the Italian daily, *La Repubblica*.[2] In the interview, Francis announced his option for a socially distanced accompaniment during the coronavirus crisis: "I will accompany you from here." "Here" presumably meant the safety and comfort of the Vatican. In a previous publication, I wrote about the impracticality and inauthenticity of accompanying vulnerable people from a distance.[3] The context of that argument was the global crisis of forced displacement of millions of refugees and the pastoral accompaniment incumbent on the community called church, especially its leaders and ministers. To protect, accompany, and advocate on behalf of refugees, the church and its ministers must be physically close to the people. They must walk with them on the path of pain and suffering of displacement:

---

[2] Paolo Rodari, "Pope Francis on Coronavirus Crisis: 'Don't Waste These Difficult Days. While at Home Re-Discover the Importance of Hugging Kids and Relatives,'" *La Repubblica*, March 18, 2020 (www.repubblica.it).

[3] Agbonkhianmeghe E. Orobator, *From Crisis to Kairos: The Mission of the Church in the Time of HIV/AIDS, Refugees and Poverty* (Nairobi, Kenya: Paulines Publications-Africa, 2005).

> For *pastoral presence* to happen, pastors and leaders would need to find the community in exile, rather than compel it to appeal repeatedly for pastoral attention. . . . Pastoral accompaniment and presence would not make sense "from a distance." They require an unambiguous option for solidarity with the people of God in exile. This "face-to-face" and "side-by-side" approach could be hugely significant from an ecclesiological point of view, especially for people afflicted by socio-political exclusion, loss of home and precarious marginal existence in a hostile environment.[4]

The force of this argumentation would seem to negate the basic option of Pope Francis to remotely accompany those infected and affected by COVID-19. However, it was written before the emergence of contagious and virulent outbreaks like Ebola Virus Disease and COVID-19, for which the standard public health advice mandates isolation, quarantine, and physical and social distancing as nonnegotiable measures of mitigation, prevention, and containment. Given this reality, pastoral accompaniment premised on physical proximity appears counterintuitive at best and dangerous at worst.

Pope Francis's approach to accompaniment in a time of crisis reveals a new way of being close. In the same interview with Rodari, Francis underscores the crucial need to "discover a new closeness," in which proximity is measured not in physical terms, but in spiritual and affective depth. This new closeness exemplifies and characterizes Pope Francis's response during the coronavirus pandemic. He reiterates his deep conviction about closeness as an expression of pastoral leadership in his interview with Austen Ivereigh: "The people of God need their pastor to be close to them, not to over-protect himself. The people of God need their pastors to be self-sacrificing."[5] There

---

[4] Ibid., 174–75.

[5] Pope Francis's interview with Austen Ivereigh, "Take Care of Yourselves for a Future That Will Come," *The Tablet* (April 11, 2020).

is a strong foundation for this ministry of consoling closeness that is not exercised exclusively as a physical experience in a time of crisis. Within the theological imagination of the pope, its source and rationale lie in the experience and promise of the Risen Christ. In Francis's two *Urbi et Orbi* blessings during the coronavirus pandemic, the theme of the presence of Jesus Christ dominated his message. At Easter, the pope reminded people reeling from the effects of a liturgical lockdown that "the Lord has not left us alone! United in our prayer, we are convinced that he has laid his hand upon us, firmly reassuring us: 'Do not be afraid, I have risen and I am with you still!'"[6]

When Francis made his aforementioned Good Friday call to the TV show *A Sua Immagine*, he did not need to introduce himself to host Lorena Bianchetti, who exclaimed excitedly, "Pope Francis! Welcome to the program!" To which Francis replied, "You recognized my voice!" This may seem a digression, but this encounter is instructive for understanding the exercise of the ministry of consolation as a way of being close to people in a time of crisis. It evokes a reassuring and comforting bond of closeness and understanding that empowers people to deal with the challenges at hand—not only physically but also spiritually. The Johannine image of the good shepherd comes to mind: "My sheep know my voice, and I know them. They follow me" (Jn 10:27). Only a leader who evinces a consoling closeness could command such a personal receptiveness from the TV host. Also pertinent is Francis's now famous principle of pastoral leadership and missionary discipleship, according to which "Evangelizers thus take on the 'smell of the sheep' and the sheep are willing to hear their voice" (*Evangelii gaudium,* 24). As a Rwandan proverb says, "If you want cows, you must sleep like a cow." Pastoral leadership in a time of crisis embodies elements of care, trust, and empathy that stem from the willingness and availability of a leader to enter into and share the condition of those whom he or she has a responsibility to serve and protect. Amid the

---

[6] Pope Francis, *Urbi et Orbi Message*, Easter 2020.

convulsion of crisis, the voice of Pope Francis exemplifies a kind of leadership that seeks out the marginalized and the vulnerable members of society in order to tend to their wounds and accompany them in their suffering.

Long before the coronavirus evolved into a global public health catastrophe, Francis's desire to exercise a consoling closeness was unequivocal: "I am close, I am close to you all." "I wish to be close to and pray for the people who are sick because of the virus that has spread through China."[7] These words of consolation were not addressed exclusively to the pope's global flock of faithful followers, but were primarily for the victims of the virus; families mourning the death of their loved ones; the health workforce of doctors, nurses, and first responders; and lay and religious ministers of women and men, sisters, and priests who did not hesitate to sacrifice their lives in the fight against COVID-19 at the frontlines, like soldiers motivated by love. Such profound desire for closeness comes from an experienced pastor endowed with a deep knowledge of people who are forced to live on the existential peripheries and the everyday heroes and heroines who dare to reach out to them with love.

Ironically, the office of consolation is not detached from the experience of desolation. The ministry of consolation is born out of a desire to enter into the experience of the suffering of people, rather than trying to evacuate suffering or its pain. In this sense, it is a manifestation of solidarity with the pain and suffering that people experience in the context of a crisis. In his encyclical letter *Sollicitudo rei socialis* (*SRS*), Pope John Paul II poignantly stated that whether as a practice or virtue, solidarity "is not a feeling of vague compassion or shallow distress at the misfortunes of so many people, both near and far. On the contrary, it is a firm and persevering determination to commit oneself to the common good; that is to say to the good of all and of each individual, because we are all really

---

[7] *A Sua Immagine*, Good Friday 2020.

responsible for all" (*SRS*, 38). Understood as such, solidarity eschews indifference and reinforces the exercise of the office of consolation, because the person who holds this office is neither averse to nor distant from the existential predicament and condition of people afflicted by crisis.

When a crisis is characterized by loss, suffering, and various forms of psychological distress, *solidarity* doubles as *empathy*, by which a person is able—literally or figuratively—to make this loss, suffering, or distress his or her own. Both qualities serve to illustrate the character of the ministry of consolation as a credible and authentic exercise that responds to people's deepest needs for comfort in a time of crisis. To recall Ignatius's idea above, the resurrected Lord exemplified a similar approach when he consoled his grieving mother. Her suffering was his suffering. As Pope Francis put it in his Palm Sunday message, on account of his solidarity and empathy with the suffering of others, "Jesus' message to us today is this: 'Do not be afraid, you are not alone. I experienced all your desolation in order to be ever close to you. . . . Courage, open your heart to my love. You will feel the consolation of God who sustains you.'"[8] The ministry of consolation is thus motivated by the practice of solidarity and empathy. The exercise of this ministry compels a leader to actively cultivate and deploy these qualities in a time of crisis through the care, support, and accompaniment of those who are most impacted by the crisis.

The kind of pastoral presence and closeness demonstrated by Pope Francis during the coronavirus crisis relies even more on concrete gestures than on effusive eloquence. When Francis spoke to Spanish journalist Jordi Evole via Skype for a Spanish TV program, the pope stressed the priority of gestures over words for people stricken and sickened by the coronavirus. "The last thing I would do is tell them something," he declared. "What I try to do is make them feel that I am close

---

[8] Pope Francis, Palm Sunday Homily, St. Peter's Basilica, April 5, 2020 (www.vaticannews.va).

to them. Today, the language of gestures is more important than words. Of course, something should be said, but it is the gesture of sending them a greeting."[9] At the time, Spain was under strict lockdown and rivaling Italy as the epicenter of the viral outbreak in Europe. Under such circumstances of widespread distress, fear, and anxiety, the pope understood that mere words are not enough; gestures of faith, hope, and love speak louder.

Whether he is reaching out to New Yorkers in lockdown, to Lorena Bianchetti, or to a frontline worker, Francis's intention is consistently focused on the well-being of the other as he seeks to express a closeness and affection that transcend the imposed and isolating abyss of social distancing. His thoughtful approach is a poignant reminder to people in the situation of crisis that they will never walk alone. For people reeling from the ravages of the coronavirus, Francis's message rarely deviates from the theme of consoling closeness and affection: "Do not forget that the pope is praying for you, he is close to you."[10] This expression of closeness and affection is a defining characteristic of the exercise of the office of consolation and a crucial component of leadership in a time of crisis. It epitomizes a way of leading from the heart, in which closeness and affection depend less on physical proximity to those who are suffering.

Compassion and Mercy as Elements of Consolation

In the preceding section, I situated the foundation of the office of consolation in the experience of the Risen Christ, and emphasized the importance of solidarity and empathy as

---

[9] Jordi Evole, "El mensaje del papa Francisco a los empresarios: 'No es momento de despedir, es momento de acoger,'" *La Vanguardia*, March 23, 2020 (www.lavanguardia.com).

[10] Pope Francis, Easter Monday Mass at Casa Santa Marta, April 13, 2020 (www.vaticannews.va).

key components in the exercise of this office. The timing of the coronavirus pandemic—paralleling the Easter season—accentuated resurrection as the dominant theme of Pope Francis's messages, reflections, and prayers in response to the crisis. This theme connects with and evokes two other key elements of the ministry of consolation, namely, compassion and mercy. Not only are these central to Francis's exercise of the office of consolation, they are also widely considered to be the defining features of his pontificate. Unsurprisingly, then, they have featured prominently in his response to the coronavirus pandemic.

Compassion

Compassion defines the capacity of people to live in difficult and challenging situations as a shared experience. In the understanding of Pope Francis, compassion "means to suffer with, to suffer together, to not remain indifferent to the pain and suffering of others."[11] As an African proverb says, "A chicken develops a headache when it sees another chicken in the cooking pot." The connection between compassion and the qualities of empathy and solidarity are striking. Compassion is not a function of whether or not all is well with me: it is about what is happening to the world, to the other. Essentially, compassion represents a summons to become affected by the shared fate of humanity and to resist the temptation of indifference. When Pope Francis addressed a group of Jesuits in October 2016, he underscored the intentional nature of compassion as a way of life. Francis declared that the cross that each person is called upon to bear and embrace may not necessarily be his or her own—the important thing is to make it one's own. Wherever there is pain, the disciples of the crucified and Risen Christ have to be present. In other words, wherever

---

[11] Pope Francis, *The Name of God Is Mercy: A Conversation with Andrea Tornielli* (New York: Random House, 2016), 91.

there is suffering, all believers are affected, because it is the Lord who is being crucified, the same Lord whom Christians are called to serve in the least of God's people.[12] On this point, it is important to eliminate any suggestion or hint of a latent glorification of suffering and pain under the guise of embracing the cross. Just as he does not minimize painful experiences, Pope Francis also does not recommend masochism as a way of life. For Francis, embracing the cross and enlisting in the discipleship of the crucified Christ derive from a deep faith in the possibility of transformation and healing. The choice of the word "possibility" is deliberate and important; there is always the risk of failure, doubt, and uncertainty, which the darkness of the coronavirus crisis accentuated for many people.

It should also be noted that not every situation of suffering makes sense. Compassion entails the willingness and capacity to persevere in embracing others in their discomfort, pain, and suffering, while always being aware of the risk of failure, doubt, and uncertainty. This implies that even if a person cannot change a situation of suffering, he or she can still choose to be there out of solidarity and with the crucified Christ who is present in the suffering of others. It is in this profound connection with the passion of Christ that the hope of defeating death lies. As Francis said in his Easter Vigil homily, repeating the lyrics of a popular song that many Italians sang from their balconies during the pandemic, it is the strong conviction that "All will be well."

As we shall see in chapter 2, compassion is the compelling motivation for venturing into the existential peripheries inhabited by the poor and the vulnerable. The implication here is that compassion does not dissolve into sentimentality—it generates the requisite passion for changing and transforming the structures that create the inequalities and inequities in the

---

[12] "Address of His Holiness Pope Francis to the 36th General Congregation of the Society of Jesus" (General Curia of the Society of Jesus, October 24, 2016).

first place. As John Paul II said regarding solidarity, compassion prioritizes the common good and the advent of a world order that creates opportunities for human flourishing without discrimination.[13] In this sense, compassion generates a moral force for radical change:

> Compassion extends beyond empathy. It does not motivate our action because we too may be harmed. Compassion motivates action because the phenomena we observe are unjust, not worthy of the world we would like to live in. . . . Compassion pushes us to understand how we have structured the world, and to ask how we can structure it better, not because we may suffer but because others are suffering and that is not how the world should be.[14]

In a time of crisis, compassion is neither a naïve sentimentality nor a pious complacency. Instead, it reflects a way of leading and a way of life that tends to the wounds of others in order to bring them consolation and to inspire a commitment to the creation of just structures and conditions of living.

Mercy

The second component of this exercise of the office of consolation is mercy. Like compassion, Pope Francis demonstrates that mercy is not an abstract word, but rather a way of life that originates in the boundless tenderness of God. The practice of mercy prioritizes action over rhetoric. Considered as a grace, mercy constitutes the locus par excellence for revealing and encountering the love and kindness of God. Mercy does not equal pity; rather, it manifests in concrete gestures

---

[13] *SRS*, 38.

[14] Sandro Galea, "Compassion in a Time of COVID-19," *The Lancet*, May 22, 2020.

that touch the lives of others in situations of brokenness and ultimately become embodied in deeds of justice. Yet, to act mercifully is neither a manifestation of willpower nor an act of voluntarism. Mercy thrives on the honest awareness of one's vulnerability and limitations in the presence of a loving and tender God.

And like compassion, mercy is not averse to suffering. In his analysis of the etymology of mercy, Francis highlights the fact that, at its root, *misericordis* "means opening one's heart to wretchedness."[15] Mercy "is the divine attitude which embraces, it is God's giving himself to us, accepting us, and bowing to forgive."[16] The pope writes,

> Mercy: the ultimate and supreme act by which God comes to meet us. Mercy: the fundamental law that dwells in the heart of every person who looks sincerely into the eyes of his brothers and sisters on the path of life. Mercy: the bridge that connects God and people, opening our hearts to the hope of being loved forever despite our sinfulness.[17]

In Francis's understanding, only a first-hand experience of God's mercy embodied in the healing power of the cross enables people to abandon the fear of allowing themselves to be moved by the immense suffering of women and men in the world. This experience of God's mercy inspires patient and compassionate accompaniment of the crucified people.

In the next chapter, I will revisit this dimension of mercy for the suffering people that forms an integral part of Pope Francis's spiritual accompaniment in the time of the coronavirus crisis. For now, the key lesson to retain is that compassion

---

[15] Francis, *The Name of God Is Mercy*, 8.
[16] Ibid., 8–9.
[17] *Misericordiae vultus*, 2.

and mercy are definitive markers of the exercise of the ministry of consolation. This ministry makes sense only as an expression of compassion and mercy freely and generously bestowed on others, especially in a time of uncertainty, suffering, and vulnerability. Mercy and compassion are two halves of a fundamental engagement inspired by a loving gaze toward, and a radical solidarity with, the vulnerable. It is an option to stand where they stand. This loving gaze and this solidarity originate in and are sustained by God's love. More importantly for this study, besides being a core element of Francis's theological imagination, mercy is in theory and practice "the defining characteristic of Pope Francis's leadership."[18] To lead in a time of crisis entails a radical manifestation of mercy, exemplified in a compassionate and tender commitment to the healing of pain and suffering and the transformation of unjust structures.

The Contagion of Hope

The coronavirus has spread with frightening speed across the world, leaving no country unaffected. By the time the World Health Organization (WHO) declared it a Public Health Emergency of International Concern, the virus had already been seeded among various global populations. And even after the WHO's declaration and concurrent warning about the virulent and insidious nature of the virus, some politicians referred to it dismissively as "a touch of flu" akin to a seasonal flu. Far from being a seasonal flu, we now know that COVID-19 is a deadly and very contagious disease in humans. Besides causing

---

[18] Marcus Mescher, "Mercy," in *Pope Francis: A Voice for Mercy, Justice, Love, and Care for the Earth,* ed. Barbara E. Wall and Massimo Faggioli (Maryknoll, NY: Orbis Books, 2019), 102–27, at 102. See Archbishop Donald Bolen, "Mercy," in *A Pope Francis Lexicon,* ed. Joshua J. McElwee and Cindy Wooden (Collegeville, MN: Liturgical Press, 2018), 127–34.

physical suffering and death, the contagion of coronavirus has also created fear, despair, uncertainty, and anxiety.

It is not unusual for leaders to respond cautiously when confronted by a crisis whose trajectory is initially largely unknown and to refrain from acting prematurely. However, while erring on the side of caution can avoid impulsive and inopportune responses, a mistimed intervention, whether deliberate or unintentional, presents the additional risk of abetting further escalation of the crisis. This pattern is certainly true of the coronavirus crisis. In addition to some leaders' denial of the gravity of the pandemic, many other leaders reacted slowly and tentatively, thus losing precious time and creating conditions for the contagion to spread along with fear, anxiety, and despair.

Set against a "contagion of despair," Pope Francis has articulated the idea of a "contagion of hope."[19] Although analogical, the latter is diametrically opposed to the former and contains nothing sinister. The viral trajectory of COVID-19 enveloped humanity in what Francis called "its darkest hour" during his near-solitary celebration of the resurrection of Jesus Christ at Easter Vigil on April 11, 2020. Contrary to this experience of confidence-shattering darkness, the contagion or gospel of hope inspires confidence and is transmitted from heart to heart. In Francis's vision, far from being a magic formula that makes problems vanish, this contagious gospel of hope is grounded in "the victory of love over the root of evil, a victory that does not bypass suffering and death, but passes through them, opening a path in the abyss, transforming evil into good: This is the unique hallmark of the power of God."[20] In this way, the pope avoids any semblance of circumventing harsh and painful realities, while affirming the primacy of life over death, light over darkness, and hope over despair as the central message in a time of crisis.

---

[19] Pope Francis, *Urbi et Orbi Message*, Easter 2020.
[20] Ibid.

Similarly, the pope distinguishes between naïve optimism, a psychological disposition that he considers superficial and fleeting, and hope, a divine gift grounded in the faith of women and men who remain purposefully committed to journeying together along the hard path of suffering, in resolute expectation that together humanity will emerge from this crisis better and stronger.[21] As he declared to Jordi Evole,

> I have hope in humanity, in men and women, and I have hope in the people. I have a lot of hope in the people who will take lessons from this crisis to rethink their lives. We are going to come out better, although there will be fewer of us, of course. Many will remain on the path and it is hard. But I have faith we will come out of this better.[22]

Most strikingly, in the context of the coronavirus crisis, Pope Francis declares hope a fundamental right. This is a novel idea that holds significant implications from the perspective of leadership. In Francis's theological imagination, in a time of crisis, human beings are "as pilgrims in search of hope"[23] in much the same way as the disciples of Jesus, especially the women, set out in the direction of the tomb of the crucified Christ. Yet hope is not only a destination, it is also the impetus for the journey. Founded on faith in the resurrection of Christ, the inalienable "right to hope," according to Francis, "is a definitive marker of a new and living hope that comes from God. It is not mere optimism; it is not a pat on the back or an empty word of encouragement. It is a gift from heaven, which we could not have earned on our own."[24] Inviting people, as

---

[21] See Natalia Imperatori-Lee, "Hope," in McElwee and Wooden, *A Pope Francis Lexicon*, 88–91.

[22] Evole, "El mensaje del papa Francisco a los empresarios."

[23] Pope Francis, Easter Vigil Homily, April 11, 2020 (www.vatican.va).

[24] Ibid.

the pope does, to embark on the arduous pilgrimage of hope in a time of crisis exemplifies a duty of leadership that contrasts sharply with the practiced penchant of some to announce a precipitous vision of light at the end of the tunnel. Spreading the contagion of hope is the crucial and solemn task of a leader in times of crisis.

In the midst of the great suffering and loss visited upon the victims of the coronavirus pandemic, the gospel of hope emerges as another important element of Pope Francis's theological vision, interior disposition, and reassuring message. This kind of hope is undimmed by the pain and suffering induced by a crisis; rather, it offers an anchor for sustaining faith and an impetus for moving forward. Asked by Lorena Bianchetti what he would be thinking about while praying the Stations of the Cross on Good Friday, Francis restated his closeness with and affection for victims of the pandemic who are suffering the most. However, the pope added that he would resist the temptation to succumb to despair amid the pain and suffering of the world. Instead, he would be "looking up, looking toward hope, because hope does not disappoint. It does not remove the pain, but it does not disappoint."[25]

In times of crisis, given their vulnerability and fragility, people look to leaders for direction, confidence, and reassurance. Yet some leaders are tempted to yield to pretense, generating misleadingly upbeat messages and offering platitudes in order to allay fears, assuage anxieties, and assure people that all is well. This kind of approach may work initially, but its deception will eventually be revealed. During a crisis, the proclamation of hope must be grounded in faith; otherwise the idea of hope serves only as a rhetorical device to numb and disguise the pain and suffering. Precisely for this reason, Francis does not separate the cross from the gospel of hope. As he stated in his March 27, 2020, prayer service at St. Peter's Basilica, "by embracing his cross" we are able "to embrace hope." The abil-

---

[25] *A Sua Immagine*, Good Friday 2020.

ity to maintain a healthy balance between the potency of hope and the reality of pain represents a critical task and gauge of authentic leadership in a time of crisis. As I have begun to demonstrate, this ability is recognizably exemplified by Pope Francis's response to the pandemic.

In the midst of such a crisis, leadership embodies closeness, empathy, compassion, and tenderness. When so many lives and livelihoods are at stake, true leadership prioritizes the well-being of others and resolutely and compassionately ministers consolation with the aim of strengthening faith, hope, and love. Interestingly, in assuming and exercising this ministry, Pope Francis neither monopolizes nor complicates it. Indeed, he implies that his ministry of consolation, along with the vocation to spread the contagion of hope, is the task of everybody. Crisis impels us to choose a new closeness as humanity in solidarity. In his interview with Paolo Rodari, Francis clearly underlines the universality and concreteness of this office of consolation. Even as the pope encourages priests to be close to the sick and isolated and to health care workers and volunteers, and to accompany them and bring the strength of the word of God to them, he insists that "Consolation must now be everyone's commitment." This consolation can be provided even in "small, concrete gestures expressing closeness and concreteness toward the people closest to us, a caress for our grandparents, a kiss for our children, for the people we love."[26] In the course of the coronavirus crisis, in all of his homilies, reflections, and allocutions, the most commonly repeated message of Pope Francis is "Do not be afraid." In this short phrase is contained the potency of compassion, mercy, and hope capable of bringing consolation to people and strengthening their capacity to confront pain and suffering in a time of crisis.

---

[26] Rodari, "Pope Francis on Coronavirus Crisis."

2

A Preference of Love

God heals the brokenhearted and binds up their
wounds.

—*Psalms 147:3*

In a 1968 letter to his order, the charismatic leader of the Jesuits, Pedro Arrupe (1907–91), coined the term "option for the
poor" to prioritize the mission of Jesuits: service of the faith,
promotion of social justice, and engagement in political action
in favor of impoverished, disempowered, and marginalized
people. Over time, the concept found enthusiastic reception in
the scholarly tradition of liberation theology in the context of
Latin America. There it was prefaced with "preferential" and
applied, to influential and contested effect. Although the idea
was initially a source of debate and controversy, it has gradually evolved and entered the mainstream theological tradition
as one of the major developments in Catholic social teaching
(CST) in the twentieth century.

Pope John Paul II accorded the term greater visibility,
acceptability, and respectability when he introduced it in his
encyclical *Centesimus annus* (1991) celebrating the centenary
of Pope Leo XIII's encyclical *Rerum novarum* (*RN*; 1891).
John Paul II also played a significant role in the development

of this concept. Notably, he expanded "option for the poor" beyond material and economic poverty to include other forms of poverty, specifically cultural and spiritual poverty. Since then, successive popes have adopted the principle of preferential option for the poor and extended its meaning to take account of a wider category of people relegated to the margins of society such as victims of ecological injustice.

Most recently, the principle has featured in the encyclicals and letters of Pope Francis as a hermeneutical tool for understanding and interpreting the interplay of social, economic, and political structures and their wider implications and impact on vulnerable populations. Construed as a theological paradigm, this principle makes a bold and radical claim. It prioritizes the dignity, needs, and rights of marginalized, disadvantaged, and vulnerable populations and assigns them the status of the privileged locus of God's revelation and the church's mission of promotion of justice.[1] This claim, which is founded on a radical reinterpretation of the life, teachings, and deeds of Jesus of Nazareth, has two implications. First, vulnerability is not a hereditary trait or a pathological defect to be accepted with an attitude of resignation. Nor do people choose to be vulnerable as one viable option among others. Rather, they are made so by a complex web of pernicious social and political structures. Second, the principle is not a supererogatory option but an ethical imperative on which depend other principles, like the common good, solidarity, and subsidiarity. In practice, it ties in closely with the qualities of compassion and mercy discussed in the previous chapter.

A contemporary and germane example of the application of the preferential option for the poor also comes from the order of the Jesuits. In February 2019, the order's superior general, Fr. Arturo Sosa, SJ, announced the outcome of a two-year process of discernment to identify the universal apostolic preferences of the Jesuits over a ten-year period. Among the

---

[1] See *Evangelii gaudium* (*EG*), 198, 123; *Laudato si'* (*LS*), 158.

four preferences selected, he listed the commitment to walk with the poor, the outcasts of the world, and those whose dignity has been violated in a mission of reconciliation and justice. Concretely, these include individuals and communities that are vulnerable, excluded, marginalized, and materially impoverished such as migrants, displaced persons, refugees, victims of wars, victims of sexual abuse, victims of human trafficking, and indigenous peoples. By making this choice, the order reaffirmed the timeless significance of this principle.

In chapter 1, I explored the exercise and practice of the office of consolation. I underscored its importance as a vital component of leadership in a time of crisis. Essential elements of this office include compassionate closeness, solidarity, mercy, and a sincere proclamation of hope. Upon even closer examination, the telos of this office or ministry is neither vague nor abstract—it is clear that Pope Francis's desire for closeness and affection has been largely focused on victims of the coronavirus, their families, and frontline workers. In this way, Francis made a preferential option for the most vulnerable and the most exposed, who are likely to catch the disease on account of their social, economic, and demographic condition or situation. This chapter examines the preferential option for the poor and vulnerable as a leadership quality in a time of crisis. It makes the point that besides *focus*, the *locus* of the leader matters in times of crisis. Where does the leader stand? Who does the leader stand with? If indeed, as we saw in the previous chapter, the ministry of consolation is exercised and expressed with closeness, affection, and solidarity, where a leader stands or with whom he or she opts to stand is also a reliable barometer of the authenticity of leadership.

This idea of locus or location is not to be confused with the habitual opportunism of politicians and partisans who use cheap photo ops to improve their favorability ratings and enhance their public appeal, even at the expense of people's suffering. In the introduction and in chapter 1, I mentioned several instances and examples of where and with whom Pope Francis stood and continues to stand in the time of crisis. To set this discussion of preferential option in context, it would help to debunk a familiar myth constructed around the coronavirus pandemic.

The Great Myth

There is no doubt about the severity of COVID-19 as a global pandemic. But one of the myths it has spawned is that it is a great social equalizer in terms of class and race, gender and age—that it affects everyone equally. This claim is problematic, as evidence seems to show that quite the opposite is true. Even though this mythical narrative makes some epidemiological sense—for example, the disease has afflicted some prominent dignitaries and celebrities, not just people who are impoverished and vulnerable—the narrative of a nondiscriminatory social and geographical disease represents a distortion of reality from a demographic and socioeconomic point of view. Generally speaking, while the occurrence of a crisis could be universal, the distribution of its negative effects may be unequal, depending on a combination of variables. Consider the coronavirus crisis: the poor do not usually travel on airplanes, and they cannot afford the luxury of vacationing on cruise ships. But when lockdowns, restrictions, and social distancing measures were imposed on vast populations, they revealed glaring disparities between the economically secure and the economically vulnerable groups in societies across the world. The latter have been more exposed to the potentially lethal virus due to unavoidable physical proximity to others in housing and working environments; not everybody enjoyed the luxury of teleworking, telehealth, and distance learning. In addition, a pandemic like COVID-19 competes with a range of other severe social crises and humanitarian emergencies. This competition could effectively reduce the comparative perception of risk associated with the disease and, therefore, undermine the degree of adherence to public health advice on preventative measures.

A familiar mantra that has been repeated across the world in relation to the coronavirus pandemic is that "We are all in this together." Not quite. Far from being the much-touted global social equalizer, the pandemic has exposed the deep economic, digital, social, racial, and ethnic fragmentation and divide in a highly networked and globalized world. In other words, rather than leveling out socioeconomic disparities, the coronavirus exposes the fault lines of society. It disproportionately affects the poorer and more vulnerable populations with preexisting or comorbid conditions, who have limited or no means to cope with or cushion its impact. The grim truth of COVID-19 is that pandemics and other crises thrive on and accentuate existing social inequalities, injustices, and polarities. They preferentially seek out the most fragile, weakest, and poorest in society. Deprived of the socioeconomic support and medical care enjoyed by an elite minority, the majority have been disproportionately impacted by the consequences of the pandemic. The key variables or determinants of this asymmetry of impact include income, social location, race, age, and ethnicity. For example, figures from a study conducted by the UK's Office for National Statistics showed that death rates from COVID-19 were proportionately higher in deprived areas compared to more affluent parts of England and Wales, by a ratio of 2:1. This reinforces the preponderance of postal code over genetic code as a determinant of the virus's interaction with the host and the outcome of the infection. When pushed to its logical conclusion, the social leveler myth of an egalitarian virus not only hides many shadows, it also distorts the way responses are generated to deal with the crisis.

There is a different way of understanding the logic of crisis as a social leveler. When Pope Francis addressed a global audience in his *Urbi et Orbi* speech of March 27, 2020, he underscored the vital interconnectedness of humanity in the face of a common enemy. To drive his message home, he adopted the metaphor of a wind-tossed boat in which all the occupants are mired in fear and painfully aware of their shared fragility, disorientation, and need for mutual comfort. Notwithstanding the pedagogical intent and appropriateness of this imagery, the fact remains that the likelihood of survival is considerably less for people at the lower rungs of the socioeconomic ladder such as low-paid workers. Here lies the paradox of a crisis like the coronavirus: many low-paid workers have been rightly hailed as frontline and essential workers during the pandemic. Francis understands this irony and thus does not relent in drawing attention to their condition, precisely to highlight the paradox of their lot in society in the midst of such a severe crisis.

We are not all in this together in the same way. Francis was forthright on this point in his March 27 reflection: "Our lives are woven together and sustained by ordinary people—often forgotten people—who do not appear in newspaper and magazine headlines nor on the grand catwalks of the latest show, but who without any doubt are in these very days writing the decisive events of our time." Francis's point underlines the impossibility of feigning indifference vis-à-vis the fate of the most vulnerable and underprivileged populations of the global community. Both before and during the pandemic, these are the people with whom the pope ordinarily associates and even socializes.

Pope Francis's nautical metaphor above contains a potent message, which is that we cannot save ourselves alone. Social, economic, or political privileges or entitlements may afford one the means to confine oneself to a safely isolated house in order to avoid contagion, but they do not confer immunity from exposure to the many cataclysmic effects of the pandemic. In other words, the accrual of social or economic advantages constitutes a weak barrier to a biological threat, especially in sprawling and densely populated urban areas—the poor and marginalized are the most vulnerable of all in terms of the initial impact of the virus, but because of the interdependence of society, nobody is safe until everybody is safe. The pertinence of this issue is reflected in the debate about vaccine nationalism and equity. In a situation where the virus is present in all parts of the world, only when vaccines become widely available and accessible will there be any guaranteed chance of bringing the pandemic under control for the entire global community. Making vaccines available to high-income populations while depriving those in low-income countries offers no lasting security. As long as the virus remains active anywhere, it will likely come back and continue to threaten the global population,[2] a point that Francis has emphasized repeatedly.[3] Francis's approach to leadership demonstrates the ethical imperative to choose to stand with the poor and vulnerable, especially in a time of crisis, with solidarity, compassion, and mercy.

Deeper Concerns for Workers

As should be obvious by now, the principle of preferential option for the poor is neither abstract nor ambiguous; the poor have faces, and their lives do not merely furnish data for statistical computation and analysis, despite a tendency to reduce them to invisibility in the calculation of global economic systems. Perhaps as never before, the coronavirus crisis has amplified the divergence between two categories of workers: those who can afford the luxury of working remotely and those who must continue to work onsite, oftentimes to sustain the structures and institutions that guarantee the privileges of the former group. Put plainly, the comfort and security of the former is often sustained by the labor and vulnerability of the latter.

Unsurprisingly, Pope Francis casts his lot with this latter category of workers. The deep concern that he expresses for

---

[2] See Gavi (Global Vaccine Alliance), "Why Is No One Safe Until Everyone Is Safe during a Pandemic?" August 17, 2020 (www.gavi.org).

[3] For example, at a Papal General Audience on August 19, 2020, Pope Francis said, "It would be sad if, for the vaccine for Covid-19, priority were to be given to the richest! It would be sad if this vaccine were to become the property of this nation or another, rather than universal and for all." http://w2.vatican.va/.

workers and for their rights and conditions is not new. Workers' rights have been a staple of CST since its inception in the nineteenth century with Pope Leo XIII's encyclical, *RN*. Nor is this concern limited to a material realm. More importantly, it opens up an essential dimension of Christian anthropology that prioritizes the inalienable dignity of the human person and the dignifying nature of human labor. The combination of rights and dignity offers a means for assessing the appalling working and living conditions of underpaid and undervalued workers, who are thus particularly at risk of being infected by COVID-19.

Of the measures that Pope Francis adopted to raise global social consciousness about the conditions for workers during the coronavirus crisis, one stands out for the brilliance and simplicity of its message. On Easter Sunday 2020, Francis drafted a letter "To our brothers and sisters of popular movements and organizations."[4] These are groups affiliated with the Vatican-sponsored annual World Meeting of Popular Movements. In the missive, the pope undertakes a brief but incisive analysis of the condition of the poor workers who are consigned to the perilous trenches and forgotten peripheries amid the chaos of crisis. Rarely recognized on account of their invisibility, they are denied access to the benefits of globalization. Without social security or guaranteed income, they live hand-to-mouth as they eke out a meager living in informal economies, consisting largely of unregulated and unprotected jobs and activities like domestic work, casual labor, and small-scale enterprises. Yet they are indispensable to the hoped-for change in the world economic order. But when pandemics strike, the poorest workers are hit twice as hard as the affluent, because the former already lack a steady income. Francis's list of vulnerable workers is long but not exhaustive—it includes street vendors, recyclers, carnies, small farmers, construction

---

[4] Pope Francis Easter Letter to World Popular Movements, Vatican City, April 12, 2020.

workers, dressmakers, bus drivers, and various categories of caregivers. They are the focus of his pastoral concern and solicitude.

The pope's advocacy and option for such workers without rights are not marked by "a feeling of vague compassion or shallow distress at the misfortunes of so many people, both near and far" (*Sollicitudo rei socialis* [*SRS*], 38). On the contrary, he proposes bold initiatives to address the urgency of their precarious existence at the margins of society in a time of crisis. To begin with, in keeping with the venerable tradition of CST, Pope Francis argues that the life and dignity of persons, communities, and peoples must be at the center of all socioeconomic and political considerations elaborated in response to the challenges of a crisis like the coronavirus pandemic. Second, neither priority nor preference for the lowest of the low represents an end in itself. As a moral framework, this principle ought to translate into concrete steps to redress situations of economic inequality and social injustice. Third, notably, Francis proposes a universal basic wage that dignifies human labor, is accessible to all, values the human person, and guarantees basic necessities for a decent living condition: "This may be the time," he writes, "to consider a universal basic wage which would acknowledge and dignify the noble, essential tasks you carry out. It would ensure and concretely achieve the ideal, at once so human and so Christian, of no worker without rights."[5]

At a deeper level of consideration, Pope Francis's concern for workers' rights does not simply expound a theoretical aspect of CST. More importantly, it is an indicator of where and with whom he stands in a time of crisis. As such, it demonstrates another aspect of good leadership, particularly at a time when the rights of vulnerable workers are ignored or violated without consideration for human dignity.

---

[5] Ibid.

At the Margins and Existential Peripheries

To reiterate a point made above, in CST, the poor and the vulnerable are not faceless realities objectified or reified in impersonal statistical computations or speculative theological and ethical disquisitions. Rather, the category of the poor and vulnerable generally comprises people who fall through the cracks of technological and economic progress and are, either structurally or systemically, marginalized or excluded from the sphere of integral human development. Also, they are systematically denied access to opportunities to improve their lot in life. In his letter to members of social movements, Pope Francis offers a succinct but sharper definition of this category of vulnerability. These are people and communities "excluded from the benefits of globalization."[6] They are accustomed to surviving on the demeaning crumbs of market solutions fabricated by others, which trickle down unevenly from the centers of economic power and political influence. They struggle to survive on the edge of social, economic, and political arrangements over which they have no control.

In the social imagination of Francis, this painful and complex reality of marginalization, exclusion, alienation, and exploitation is rendered as "existential peripheries."[7] These edges of society are collateral damage caused by the asymmetries and polarities of societal power, privilege, and influence. By nature, peripheries span geographical, sociological, economic, and demographic spaces. Qualifying peripheries as existential implies that inhabiting those spaces adversely affects the entire scope of existence of people whose capacity to flourish is limited, curtailed, and impeded by systemic structures and mechanisms designed to maintain and extract benefit from such arrangements.

---

[6] Ibid.

[7] "Havana Prelate Shares Notes from Cardinal Bergoglio's Pre-Conclave Speech," March 26, 2013 (www.zenit.org).

Yet, the notion of peripheries defines more than an impregnable reality of confinement, isolation, and exclusion. As Massimo Faggioli demonstrates brilliantly in *The Liminal Papacy of Pope Francis*, "In Francis's imagination the border is more a *limen* (threshold) than a *limes* (rigid frontier). The concept of liminality is key to understanding Francis's pontificate because of his reinterpretation of the borders in the age of new walls. It's a border that relates and connects the 'other' more than it excludes."[8] In its originality, Francis's focus on thresholds rather than walls defines a clear goal of making a preferential option for the poor. Accordingly, while admitting the existence of peripheries, Francis's ultimate intention and purpose is to breach their artificial borders and relocate the focus of society and the church to those peripheral and marginal spaces. Put differently, the aim is to situate the church and society within this locus. In this sense, existential peripheries are deeply anthropological and spiritual. Although real and concrete, for the pope, existential peripheries are rendered invisible by attitudes of indifference, forgetfulness, and self-centeredness. In his interview with Jordi Evole, Pope Francis describes those at the peripheries as "people who we only know as a concept."[9] It is to their space that Francis has repeatedly and insistently invited the church to relocate and direct its missionary focus, as recorded in his now famous allocution prior to his election as pope: "The Church is called to come out of herself and to go to the peripheries not only in the geographic sense but also the existential peripheries: those of the mystery of sin, of pain, of injustice, of ignorance, of doing without religion, of thought and of all misery."[10] The upshot of the pope's prefer-

---

[8] Massimo Faggioli, *The Liminal Papacy of Pope Francis: Moving toward Global Catholicity* (Maryknoll, NY: Orbis Books, 2020), 3.

[9] Jordi Evole, "El mensaje del papa Francisco a los empresarios: 'No es momento de despedir, es momento de acoger,'" *La Vanguardia*, March 23, 2020 (www.lavanguardia.com).

[10] "Havana Prelate Shares Notes."

ence is an ecclesiological imagination of a church that resists the temptation to indulge in a self-referential narcissism and that goes forth, albeit "bruised, hurting and dirty because it has been out on the streets, rather than a Church which is unhealthy from being confined and from clinging to its own security" (*EG*, 49). Such a community or society delineates a space where the poor and vulnerable find hospitality, dignity, and solidarity, because it is "a Church which is poor and for the poor" (*EG*, 198).

In opting preferentially for the poor and vulnerable in a time of crisis, Pope Francis invokes this notion of existential peripheries to plead their cause and advocate for them. In so doing, he locates himself firmly within this space. He stands where they stand. A deep analysis of his reflections, messages, and gestures during the coronavirus crisis reveals the categories of people at the margins or existential peripheries who occupy preferentially the attention, concern, and affection of Francis. To put it in colloquial terms, these are the people that the pope prefers to hang out with.

Refugees and Migrants

Pope Francis's personal closeness to and affection for migrants and refugees is well documented. From the Island of Lampedusa (Italy) of the Mediterranean to the Island of Lesbos (Greece) on the Aegean, Francis has consistently and forcefully lent his moral voice to advocate for urgent concerted efforts to avoid the recurrence of tragedies that befall migrants and refugees in situations of crisis. As he said of Lampedusa after the drowning and death of hundreds of migrants in the Mediterranean, they "are men and women like us, our brothers and sisters seeking a better life; starving, persecuted, wounded, exploited, victims of war; they are seeking a better life. They were seeking happiness."[11]

---

[11] Pope Francis, Regina Caeli address, Saint Peter's Square, April 19, 2015 (www.vatican.va).

While previous popes have raised their voices on behalf of displaced and migratory peoples, none have done so with the personal conviction and passion of Pope Francis. His approach is as straightforward as it is compelling. One example that comes to mind is his proposal of an ethical solution to the international management of migration. Francis articulates it by four verbs: *welcome, protect, promote, and integrate.*[12] In the pope's understanding, a generous approach of *welcoming* those who knock at our doors is the direct antithesis of attitudes of rejection and indifference that cause individuals, communities, and societies to undermine the dignity of people on the move. This attitude of welcome consists in part of opening accessible, legal, and secure humanitarian channels for migration. Francis understands that migrants are essentially vulnerable persons whose rights and dignity are at risk of being ignored or violated. Migratory experiences expose people to vulnerabilities. Moreover, migrants face multiple exploitations and abuses, including hostilities of unwelcoming governments and exploitation by organized criminal groups. Accordingly, he argues, the responsibility to *protect*

> is a moral imperative which translates into adopting juridical instruments, both international and national, that must be clear and relevant; implementing just and far reaching political choices; prioritizing constructive processes, which perhaps are slower, over immediate results of consensus; implementing timely and humane programs in the fight against "the trafficking of human flesh"; which profits off others.[13]

A logical outcome of protection is the *promotion* of the integral development of migrants, exiles, and refugees in a

---

[12] Pope Francis, "Address to International Forum on Migration and Peace," February 21, 2017 (www.zenit.org).

[13] Ibid.

manner that allows them access to the social goods necessary for human flourishing. As to the responsibility to *integrate*, rather than merely assimilating or incorporating migrants into the host and dominant culture—or, worse still, relegating migrant communities to impenetrable ghettoes—integration entails a mutuality that recognizes the humanity of the weak and the "cultural richness" they possess that would positively complement the development of their adopted home. This last point is the most important component of the pope's approach, namely, the recognition of the mutuality of hospitality. It implies that a guest does not always come as a burden; he or she comes also with gifts and values to share with the host and to enhance the latter's life. As a Swahili proverb says, "A visitor is a guest for two days; on the third day, put him or her to work." So doing, the guest begins to contribute to the social and economic well-being of the host household and community. On a theological level, Francis has argued that like other vulnerable populations, displaced people serve a salvific purpose—they are manifestations of a transformative encounter with the resurrected Lord.

> In the faces of the hungry, the thirsty, the naked, the sick, strangers and prisoners, we are called to see the face of Christ who pleads with us to help (cf. Mt 25:31–46). If we can recognize him in those faces, we will be the ones to thank him for having been able to meet, love and serve him in them. Displaced people offer us this opportunity to meet the Lord.[14]

This approach is consistent with preferential love as a key determinant of the location or positioning of leadership.

Going further, Pope Francis invites people of goodwill, individually and collectively, to conjugate "these four verbs, in

---

[14] Message of His Holiness Pope Francis for the 106th World Day of Migrants and Refugees 2020 (September 27, 2020), issued May 13, 2020.

the first person singular and in the first person plural," that is, "I/we welcome, protect, promote, integrate." Such an exercise is not a grammatical gimmick—the moral lexicon proposed by Francis contains a responsibility and duty of care toward women and men who, for various reasons, have been forced to leave their homeland—a duty of justice, civility, and solidarity.[15] These attitudes and approaches become vitally important during a pandemic, particularly when the fear of physical proximity serves as an excuse to reject, exclude, isolate, or victimize the stranger. Denied food, social support, and access to health care facilities, migrants and refugees living in crowded shelters or detention centers, makeshift camps, or in the streets risk further exposure to a contagious and deadly virus. This convergence of factors and conditions of living places them in the rank of the most vulnerable and disempowered people in society. For people living on the margins of society in a time of crisis, like refugees, migrants, and the homeless, Francis's concern seems quite basic, as is clear in his Easter *Urbi et Orbi* message: "Let us ensure that they do not lack basic necessities such as medicine and especially the possibility of adequate health care."[16]

Prisoners and Detainees

Across the world, prisoners are rarely accorded any priority. They are considered social outcasts who are better kept out of sight and out of mind. Yet an early realization by governments and civic authorities was the high risk of infection among prisoners and detainees by COVID-19 on account of their confined space, which renders social distancing, self-isolation, and personal hygiene impracticable. Under these circumstances, the strident tone of an assessment by a coalition of US Catholic leaders is hardly surprising: "We are deeply

---

[15] Francis, "Address to International Forum on Migration and Peace."

[16] Pope Francis, *Urbi et Orbi Message*, Easter 2020.

concerned that experiencing COVID-19 from behind bars could, for some, mean a *de facto* death sentence."[17] Prison occupancy rates almost always exceed stated capacity, which, in addition to unsanitary conditions, makes prisons hotspots for contagion and infection during a pandemic.

As a newly ordained priest, I had the privilege of presiding regularly over Eucharistic celebrations at a local jailhouse in Benin City, Nigeria. The overcrowding in the cells was visibly inhumane. But that was not the only problem. Besides food, which was perpetually in short supply and of appalling quality, the item that inmates craved most was a bar of medicated soap to deal with the permanent outbreak of contagious skin diseases like scabies. Early on in the coronavirus pandemic, on March 29, 2020, Pope Francis made a passionate appeal on behalf of prisoners and detainees about a looming tragedy should the coronavirus take hold among those incarcerated in overcrowded prisons.[18] He also highlighted the fact that in the time of the coronavirus pandemic, inmates experienced isolation from their loved ones who were not allowed to visit them. Fittingly, many countries released significant numbers of detainees and prisoners. For example, to curb the spread of the coronavirus among incarcerated people, Iran released 85,000 prisoners, while France, Italy, and Rwanda reduced their prison populations by 10,000, 6,000, and 3,500, respectively. At various times, the pope offered prayers for—and expressed his closeness to and affection for—prisoners and detainees who suffer because of the uncertainty of conditions inside the prisons and concern about their families outside of prison. Francis's concern for prisoners and detainees was poignantly enacted during the *Via Crucis* ("Way of the Cross" or "Stations of the Cross") that he presided over on Good Friday 2020 from the steps of St. Peter's Basilica, in full view of a global TV and social media audience.

---

[17] "Statement of Solidarity: A Catholic Response to COVID-19 behind Bars," May 19, 2020 (www.catholiccharitiesusa.org).

[18] Pope Francis, Angelus Address, March 29, 2020 (www.vatican.va).

The liturgical event was led by two groups. The first group represented prisoners and detainees from the *Due Palazzi* House of Detention located in Padua, northern Italy; the second group was made up of health care workers. Carrying the cross in relay, members of the prisoners' group offered reflections, prayers, and meditations corresponding to a particular station of the cross. Strikingly, the focus extended beyond prisoners and detainees; it encompassed their wider existential world, namely, their families; the victims and families of victims; correctional officers; and all who are involved in the criminal justice system. Equally extraordinary was the fact that the meditations were not recited from stock devotional material but were composed by people from the parish of *Due Palazzi*, which included prisoners, victims, guards, families, judges, a priest, and others associated with the prison. Although I recount this event here to emphasize the practice of a preferential love for the vulnerable and weakest members of society, it had an even wider significance. After the event, Pope Francis sent a message of gratitude to participants thanking them for their contribution to the Way of the Cross that he walked with them. Francis addressed them as "friends" and reassured them of his care, compassion, and closeness: "I carry you always in my heart. Thank you."[19] Such an expression of gratitude and use of the term of affection, "friends," are not normally featured in discourse about prisoners and detainees.

The pope's affection and concern for the plight of prisoners in the global criminal justice system takes on a new significance in the context of a public health crisis. In the context of the coronavirus pandemic that rendered them particularly vulnerable, the pope chose to draw the world's attention to the people dwelling in the existential peripheries of corrections to ensure that their story and their faith, hope, and love are not

---

[19] Message of His Holiness Pope Francis to the Parish of the "Due Palazzi" Detention Centre in Padua, Good Friday, April 10, 2020 (www.vatican.va).

drowned in what he called a "sea of anonymity."[20] It takes the perspicacity and humanity of a leader in the manner of Pope Francis to notice and highlight this detail in a time of crisis.

Everyday Heroes

On Palm Sunday 2020, Pope Francis celebrated the customary Eucharistic liturgy with only a handful of people in St. Peter's Basilica. In his homily, Francis uttered these poignant words: "Dear friends, look at the real heroes who come to light in these days. They are not famous, rich and successful people; rather, they are those who are giving themselves in order to serve others."[21] From the foregoing paragraphs and what is now known about the coronavirus pandemic, it is not hard to guess the identity of these real heroes and heroines.

In addition to the group representing prisoners and detainees in the Good Friday liturgy in St. Peter's Basilica mentioned above, the second group represented health care personnel: doctors, nurses, first responders, and caregivers. As in other parts of the world, Francis recognized and praised them as the real heroes and heroines, soldiers of love, and frontline soldiers. He noted that they are vulnerable to but not deterred by a potentially lethal virus. Along with those at the existential peripheries, these people also constitute the focus of his preferential attention, closeness, and affection. In a special way, the pope linked the plight of people sickened by COVID-19 to the heroism and sacrifice of health care workers. The latter courageously give their lives in service of the former, as he pointed out in his introduction to the Eucharist in the chapel at Casa Santa Marta on March 18, 2020. At an earlier General Audience on Wednesday, March 11, 2020, livestreamed from the Library of the Apostolic Palace, the pope was more direct and

---

[20] Ibid.

[21] Pope Francis, Palm Sunday Homily, St. Peter's Basilica, April 5, 2020 (www.vaticannews.va).

vocal about the vital link between the sick and their caregivers, as well as the gratitude owed to the latter:

> Right now, I would like to speak directly to all those ill with the coronavirus, who are suffering from this sickness, and to the many people suffering uncertainty related to their own illnesses. I offer my heartfelt thanks to hospital personnel, doctors, nurses, and volunteers who in this difficult moment are close to people who are suffering.

These people, he reiterated, are close to his heart. He knows and feels their pain. More will be said about this category of heroes and heroines in the next chapter.

We Old People

There is one more vulnerable group of people worth mentioning for whom Pope Francis not only expresses a preference of love but also to which he belongs: the elderly. Francis has demonstrated a particular concern for this demographic group, not only on account of their fragility, vulnerability, and susceptibility to the coronavirus but also because of the associated challenges of loneliness, isolation, depression, and abandonment. Their age makes them vulnerable and their preexisting conditions predispose them to the worst outcomes of COVID-19. The age-related mortality of the coronavirus pandemic has raised alarm in some countries in Europe, where the WHO estimated that approximately 50 percent of the deaths may have taken place in nursing homes and assisted-living facilities. The lay Catholic Community of Sant'Egidio has spoken trenchantly of "humanly and juridically unacceptable" "sacrifice" and "sad stories of the massacres of elderly people in institutions."[22] This vulnerable demographic was the special

---

[22] "There Is No Future without the Elderly: Appeal to Re-Humanize

focus of Pope Francis in his homily on April 15, 2020: "We pray today for the elderly, especially those who are isolated or in retirement homes. . . . They are afraid, afraid of dying alone. They experience this pandemic as something aggressive against them." Tellingly, at eighty-three years of age, not only does Francis belong to this most vulnerable demographic, he has advocated repeatedly for a culture of appreciation, care, and compassion for the elderly. In one of his catecheses on aging, Pope Francis admits that "We old people are all a little fragile." More importantly, he declares that

> In a civilization in which there is no room for the elderly or where they are thrown away because they create problems, this society carries with it the virus of death. . . . We must reawaken the *collective sense of gratitude*, of appreciation, of hospitality, which makes the elder feel like a living part of his/her community. . . . Where there is no honour for the elderly, there is no future for the young.[23]

The rationale for Pope Francis's preferential option of love for this group of fellow old people in a time of crisis seems to me compelling enough that it does not need further elaboration.

"I am thinking of the many people who are weeping. . . . Many people are weeping. We, too, from our hearts, accompany them. Indeed, it wouldn't do us any harm to weep a bit as our Lord wept for all of his people." With these words, Pope Francis began the Eucharist in the chapel at Casa Santa Marta, on March 23, 2020. Although the force of the point that I make in this chapter about the focus of the pope does not lie in numbers, we can cite many more examples of the groups that have been the subject of Pope Francis's preferential concern,

---

Our Societies. No to a Selective Healthcare System," May 28, 2020 (www.santegidio.org).

[23] Pope Francis, General Audience, March 4, 2015 (www.vatican.va).

solidarity, and love in the time of the coronavirus pandemic. These are the people whom he chooses to stand and weep with figuratively and literally. In keeping with the premise of this chapter, the above sampling demonstrates the significance of the location of leadership in a time of crisis. By drawing global attention to the plight of the vulnerable and to ethical questions spawned by the coronavirus pandemic in his prayers, reflections, appeals, messages, and actions, Francis demonstrates that compassion, empathy, and solidarity with the poor and the vulnerable count as the hallmark of authentic leadership, especially in times of uncertainty and crisis. In articulating his concern for the poor and vulnerable, Francis is fully aware that, without exception, all of them are disadvantaged, at risk, and exposed to dire consequences of the global public health crisis. The principal lesson here is that their situation or location means that they hold an unquestioned primacy and priority in the exercise of the personal and collective duty and responsibility of love, care, and justice.[24] These are the crucified people whom Francis spoke about on Lorena Bianchetti's Good Friday television show,[25] who had been weighing on his mind and with whom he stands on account of a preference of love.

---

[24] See *SRS*, 42.

[25] On Good Friday 2020, Francis called in and spoke to host Lorena Bianchetti of *A Sua Immagine* (In His Image) on Italy's Rai 1 channel.

3

Celebrating Goodness

God will rejoice over you with gladness, and will
renew you in love; God will exult over you with
loud singing as on a day of festival.

—*Zephaniah 3:17–18*

The previous chapter focused on the preference of love for the
poor and the vulnerable, which manifests as a prioritization
of the needs of people situated in precarious spaces that are
designated as existentially marginal and peripheral. Part of the
essence of leadership in a time of crisis resides in the intentional refocusing of attention on these spaces as a preferential option motivated by solidarity, empathy, compassion, and
mercy. From this perspective, the choice to stand with the poor
and the vulnerable signals a leader's desire to experience their
suffering in a tangible way and to feel with empathy what it
is like to be in their shoes. Also, this choice implies an ethical
imperative to remedy and transform structures of inequality,
inequity, and injustice.

This chapter continues the discussion by making the argument that if the preferential option prioritizes dignity, rights,
and justice for people, part of this process derives from and
entails a recognition and celebration of the inherent goodness

43

of humanity. Just as pandemics can test faith and assault hope, they can also undermine belief in this goodness. The sadness and gloom of a crisis can eclipse the light of human goodness as one of its casualties. To recognize, appreciate, and celebrate goodness is to valorize human dignity and avoid treating it as inevitable, epidemiological collateral damage in the battle against a ferocious and deadly virus. In a time of crisis, it takes a conscientious and compassionate leader to keep watch over human dignity with vigilance when it is threatened by political expediency or economic calculation.

Across the world, despite the crushing and demoralizing effects of the coronavirus pandemic, there still remains an acknowledgment of the goodness of humanity. There is ample evidence of a heightened sense and display of empathy, compassion, and solidarity triggered by the realization of the interconnectedness of humanity's predicament in the face of a global public health threat. Quite clearly, the light of goodness has survived the plague's assault and has remained undimmed by the darkness of death, despair, and fear. Pope Francis offers concrete examples of how to be prophetic in encouraging and upholding confidence in the inherent goodness of humanity as well as celebrating it in a time of crisis. The importance of this aspect of his leadership can hardly be overstated at a time when many countries have experienced the effects of ill-prepared leaders, lack of adequate resources, and health care systems on the brink of being overwhelmed by the sheer numbers of cases and fatalities. In such situations, never has the manifestation of human goodness been a greater asset. It is not an exaggerated claim that the goodness of so many people serves as the vital thread that has held a fragile world together. More importantly, it is undeniable that the multiple forms of sacrifice or risk by health care workers and a multitude of essential workers on behalf of their fellow countrywomen and countrymen have effectively helped to stave off the worst effects of the virus.

Flowers of Hope

In a certain sense, there is nothing particularly unique to Pope Francis when it comes to celebrating goodness in the time of the coronavirus outbreak. Across the world, there have been multiple examples of such celebration in the numerous ways that people expressed gratitude to workers on the front line in the fight against COVID-19. Some celebrations were spontaneous and simple; others were choreographed and at times controversial. These morale-boosting events showed profound appreciation and gratitude for the heroic commitment and sacrifice of so many frontline and essential workers. In India, the country's military took to the skies to thank health care workers by raining down a floral tribute on them from a helicopter. Similarly, in other cities, airplanes staged colorful flypasts to honor health care workers. In one US city, police officers parked patrol cars in a heart formation to show appreciation. A group hosted a prayer vigil for health care professionals in a carpark outside a US hospital, while on Broadway people were serenaded by celebrities singing in tribute to frontline health care workers.

The most common form of tribute was clapping. A daily clapping took place in New York City at 7 p.m. In French cities, residents clapped daily at 8 p.m. The most notable clapping tribute was "Clap for Our Carers" in the UK. This campaign brought British citizens out onto their balconies, doorsteps, windows, and gardens every Thursday at 8 p.m. to publicly applaud the National Health Service (NHS) doctors, nurses, cleaners, and other health care staff on the front lines of the battle against the coronavirus. It was launched by Dutch Londoner Annemarie Plas, who drew inspiration from her experience of a similar tribute to health workers in her native country, the Netherlands. This weekly event afforded many people across the UK an opportunity to deliver a touching message of appreciation for the heroism and goodness of health care staff and other key workers at the forefront of the fight to save lives and defeat a common and lethal enemy. With clapping events in the UK, Canada, France, Italy, Spain, the Netherlands, India, and other countries, citizens under nationwide lockdown and isolation paid stirring tributes to health care workers with cheering, singing, dancing, and banging of pots and pans.

In the same spirit of appreciation, some landmarks and monuments have been illuminated across the world. Notably, in Rio de Janeiro, the iconic Christ the Redeemer statue was lit up on Easter Sunday with images of medical professionals wearing scrubs and putting on face masks to pay tribute to frontline health workers in Brazil and across the world. Messages of thanks in various languages and flags from different countries with the word "Hope" were also projected during the event. Across the globe, countless murals have been created in public buildings and spaces featuring health care workers on the front lines during the COVID-19 pandemic.

In Kenya, where the flower-growing industry was decimated by the coronavirus pandemic, local growers started a campaign christened "Flowers of Hope." Cut flowers is Kenya's second most important export commodity, representing 16 percent of the total. Rather than watch their produce rot, the growers sent cut flowers to local hospitals to thank and encourage hospital staff. The initiative gained a high profile when Kenya's president, Uhuru Kenyatta, decided to spread the cheer and extend the gesture abroad. With his endorsement, a flower consignment of three hundred bouquets of roses was flown by Kenyan Airways to the UK and distributed to National Health Service workers on the front lines of the pandemic as well as to patients and residents of care homes. Each bouquet carried a message of goodwill from Kenyatta on behalf of Kenyans: "Whatever the adversity, no matter the foe, we shall triumph together." Considering that the UK is one of the largest importers of cut flowers from Kenya, the political and economic subplot was not lost on Kenyans. Critics accused the government of failing to attend to the needs of Kenyan workers, especially those on the front line in the fight against the pandemic. In his defense, the president claimed that the flowers were sent to the UK to bring joy and show solidarity with frontline health workers fighting the pandemic. More crucially, though, he conceded the strategic intent of the floral largess on a nationwide TV broadcast: "When we send those flowers [to the UK] and they see they are coming from Kenya, when markets get back to operation and people go to trade they will see our flowers and remember that we thought of them when they were in trouble and that goodwill will prompt them to buy our flowers. They say friends remember each other during trouble."[1] The timing of this presidential initiative coincided with the worst period in the rate of infection and the tally of fatalities in Britain due to COVID-19.

These acts of appreciation and gratitude have a wider implication for the subject of this book. Amid the devastation of the virus, there is still something to celebrate. More accurately, there are people to celebrate—their generosity, goodwill, and goodness. The exercise of leadership in a time of crisis bears the responsibility for providing this reminder—in his messages and reflections during the coronavirus crisis, Pope Francis has consistently focused attention on the good and light that can come out of a situation of evil and darkness. It takes sensitivity and consciousness to celebrate this goodness in the people who embody and exemplify it. Celebrating goodness counts as a component of compassionate and conscientious leadership in a time of crisis. It goes beyond simply crafting words of encouragement and showing appreciation, though these are important gestures. The celebration of goodness draws on a profound recognition of the finest manifestations of the human spirit and the people who sustain this spirit

---

[1] "Think before You Start Talking Nonsense—Uhuru Finally Explains Why He Sent Flower Gifts to UK," *Pulse Live*, May 1, 2020 (www.pulselive.co.ke).

even at the lowest ebb of crisis. It comes from a depth of faith in the inherent goodness of humanity. Instances of this celebration of goodness abound, but a few will suffice here for the purposes of illustration and analysis.

Humanity That Warms the Heart

As mentioned, frontline health care workers and essential workers hold a place of pride among the people who have exemplified the finest manifestations of the human spirit during the coronavirus pandemic. Included in the list of those people whom he identifies as "crucified people," Pope Francis regularly mentions "the doctors, nurses, religious sisters, priests who have died on the frontlines like soldiers." Francis reserves evocative epithets for them, notably "soldiers of love" and "bedside angels." He has lauded them as "pastor doctors" and "good shepherds" who, like Jesus Christ, lay down their lives to save others. On June 20, 2020, when Francis spoke to a group of doctors, nurses, and health care workers from the corona-ravaged Italian region of Lombardy, he referred to them as "a visible sign of humanity that warms the heart" and "silent craftsmen [and craftswomen] of the culture of closeness and tenderness." He said affectionately, "Dear doctors and nurses, the world was able to see the good you have done in a time of great challenge. Though tired, you continued to commit yourselves with professionalism and self-sacrifice."[2] By now, such effusiveness should hardly be surprising. Gratitude, appreciation, affection, and recognition are the dominant terms in the pope's vocabulary when he speaks of doctors and nurses and people who provide critical services. These are the people who risk their lives to care for the sick and to ease the pain, difficulties, and sufferings caused by the pandemic.

---

[2] "Pope Thanks Italian Doctors and Health Care Workers for Heroic Service during Pandemic," *Vatican News*, June 20, 2020 (www.vaticannews.va).

They also include people who work in service, hospitality, transportation, agricultural, education, and courier sectors. To designate them as essential implies that society depends on them in order to function; they are indispensable, and they are rarely if ever able to work from the comfort and safety of their homes. As Pope Francis said on March 27, they "are in these very days writing the decisive events of our time."[3] Ironically, they face two severe threats: first, their work carries a disproportionately higher risk of exposure to the virus and, second, their socioeconomic status rarely affords them the means for adequate remuneration, social security, and health insurance.

Pope Francis views medical personnel as people who empty themselves out to care for and save the lives of the sick and their families, at great risk to their own lives. Whenever he mentions the heroic service of doctors, nurses, and other medical workers, he reserves a prayer for them. Most frequently, he has invoked the intercession of the Virgin Mary and the intercession of his favorite saint, Joseph, for their protection, as I will show in the next chapter. Besides choosing to put other people's lives before their own, several factors make the service of health care workers intensely challenging, terrifying, and perilous and their conduct exceptionally edifying, gracious, and audacious. Stories abound of medical personnel facing extremely stressful and upsetting situations due to overwhelming numbers of cases of infection and elevated fatalities. This emotionally exhausting situation is compounded by the pandemic's strain on health care facilities and infrastructure, as frequently evidenced by shortages of health care personnel and critical supplies like personal protective equipment, ventilators, and testing kits. These conditions put medics at a high risk of catching the virus. The combination of these factors triggered another exasperating situation, namely, the burden of making decisions of an ethical nature with consequential implications

---

[3] "Extraordinary Moment of Prayer Presided Over by Pope Francis," Friday, March 27, 2020 (www.vatican.va).

for their patients. The coronavirus pandemic compelled some doctors and nurses to make agonizing decisions about whose lives to prioritize, especially when life-saving equipment like ventilators and respirators were in limited supply. And one of the worst factors making frontline workers' jobs dangerous was the spread of misinformation driven by fear, stigma, and blame of doctors and nurses as vectors of coronavirus in some parts of the world. There were appalling incidents of violence against health care workers and stigmatization of people with, or suspected of having, COVID-19. Given these circumstances, depicting these health care workers as soldiers in a field of battle fighting to save lives from a highly contagious and deadly virus at the expense of their own neither exaggerates nor mischaracterizes their heroic service and sacrifice.

Two vignettes (among many) conclude this section on Pope Francis's outreach to frontline workers and his penchant for celebrating the goodness of people, especially health care workers. The first is a widely featured story of a Congolese nun, Dr. Angel Bipendu. A member of the Sisters of the Redeemer, Dr. Bipendu worked on the front line of the coronavirus crisis as part of a special care unit specifically responsible for visiting the homes of COVID-19 patients in the hard-hit Italian city of Bergamo. She explained the motivation behind her service as a nun and a medical doctor:

> Seeing there were many doctors who were sick, many doctors who died, there were many patients who had no help and who had no follow-up, that's why I said I'm going to give something away too. God has given me a gift; it is time now that I can give back what God has given me. . . . By giving my life to others, I also accepted to be a doctor to help those who need me even more.[4]

---

[4] Magdalene Kahiu, "'It Is Time to Give Back What God Has Given Me': Congolese Nun at Italian COVID-19 Centre," *ACI Africa*, April 19, 2020 (www.aciafrica.org).

This soldier of love expressed a sentiment with which Pope Francis would undoubtedly have concurred, and which he would have celebrated as a genuine mark of the goodness that resides at the core of humanity.

The second story concerns a handwritten letter sent by Pope Francis in April 2020 to the personnel of Spallanzani Hospital in Rome, which specializes in infectious diseases and the treatment of coronavirus patients. In his typically warm and affectionate style, Francis expressed his heartfelt gratitude for their workers' generosity and "living witness" and expressed his closeness to them: "I know all that the doctors, nurses, porters and administrative staff are doing. I know that their generosity has no limits . . . I would like these lines to make me present among you, to say with you all: only together will we make it. Thank you, thank you very much!"[5] The pope's choice of words brings to mind the Johannine imagery of a shepherd who knows his or her sheep and whose voice is recognized by them.

His message of sincere gratitude and appreciation calls to mind a similar one from a political leader, Prime Minister Jacinda Ardern of New Zealand, albeit in a different circumstance. When she placed New Zealanders on lockdown on March 21, 2020, in a televised nationwide address, her action represented an unprecedented measure that was bound to significantly disrupt the lives of the citizens. Yet her message was remarkable for the way it radiated compassion, empathy, clarity, and honesty. It bore the hallmarks of a spontaneous, heartfelt address to her people that recognized and appreciated their goodness. Above all, she showed gratitude and thanked goodhearted New Zealanders for all that they were about to do. Her words showed that her gratitude for the collective daily sacrifices to come was genuine; it was neither contrived nor an afterthought. The pope and the prime minister have exemplified

---

[5] Posted on the hospital's official Twitter account (@INMISpallanzani) on April 17, 2020.

the importance of gratitude and appreciation incarnated in words and gestures as a way to celebrate the inherent goodness of people in the midst of a crisis.

Custodians of a Flame of Mercy

As should be clear by now, when celebrating goodness and showing gratitude and appreciation, Pope Francis does not see an undifferentiated mass of people. It is part of his genius that he is also able to single out particular individuals and groups for recognition, praise, and appreciation. Perhaps this comes naturally to a pope renowned for his ability to spot a baby, a special-needs child, or the badly deformed face of a sick person in a sea of people—and to embrace each one of them with affection. Sifting through his reflections, prayers, allocutions, and messages reveals that Francis celebrates women particularly—in their respective roles, duties, and professions—as the embodiment of goodness in the time of the coronavirus crisis. For Francis, the efforts of so many women during the pandemic to take care of other people as doctors, nurses, members of security forces, prison guards, and employees in stores providing basic necessities, offer a practical demonstration of the commandment to love as God loves with self-sacrificing love, tenderness, and compassion.

Quite intentionally, Francis compliments this group of women in his inspirational exegesis of postresurrection narratives. His Easter Vigil homily insightfully draws parallels between the experience of the women in Jerusalem, after the crucifixion of Jesus of Nazareth, and all the women on the front lines in a world caught in the throes of a ravaging virus. The anxious time in which the global population waits in hope for a new dawn devoid of the pandemic and a return to normal life mirrors the Jerusalem women's impatient wait for dawn to break in order to set out on the path that leads to the tomb where Jesus was buried. In the deafening silence of Holy Saturday these women had become the main cast in

the drama of suffering, unexpected tragedy, and death that
threw a pall of thick darkness over their hearts. Their pain
and apprehension about their fate and future resembled the
condition of a world struggling to catch a glimmer of hope
amidst the grimness of the pandemic. Faced with the enormity
and gravity of the situation, the temptation of retreating into
the safe (albeit paralyzing) zone of fear, regret, and self-pity
was real for these women in Nazareth. Yet, declared Francis,
"they did not stop loving; in the darkness of their hearts, they
lit a flame of mercy."[6] They carried on with their preparation
of spices to anoint the body of Jesus, unwittingly betokening
the "'dawn of the first day of the week,' the day that would
change history." Impelled by their intense witness of prayer
and love, and heedless of the danger that loomed ominously in
the half-lit dawn, they set out to tend to the body of the crucified Lord, "like a seed buried in the ground," and, in so doing,
helped "to make new life blossom, and hope flower." Such is
the power of their hope that it continues to inspire their prog-
enies right up to this time of crisis. For Francis, these women
of the resurrection are the legitimate fore-mothers of the many
women who continue to risk their lives by tending to the sick
and afflicted and the infected and the affected, ministering to
them undeterred by the dread of a lethal virus. "Likewise, in
today's pandemic-haunted world, how many people, in these
sad days, have done and are still doing what those women did,
sowing seeds of hope! With small gestures of care, affection
and prayer."

However, it should be said that not everybody is per-
suaded by Pope Francis's insight. For all the brilliance of
Francis's exegetical prowess, as evident in his praise for the
women of Jerusalem, he has on many occasions found himself in the crosshairs of a long-standing controversy over
the status of women in the Catholic Church. On this issue,

---

[6] Homily of His Holiness Pope Francis, Holy Saturday, April 11,
2020 (www.vatican.va).

Francis's pontificate has been viewed with a disaffection and disillusionment that borders on obsession by those who believe that he has dragged the church too far away from its original identity rooted in a clerically dominated hierarchy, in contrast with others who are irked by what they believe to be a deliberate, even disingenuous, foot-dragging and inaction regarding long-overdue reform of the role and participation of women in ecclesial ministry and leadership. Yet to an exceptional degree and to his credit, Pope Francis's approach would seem to exemplify a theological acumen that supersedes the narrow agendas of both groups of combative ideological crusaders. The critical difference seems to be Francis's singular ability to focus on the enduring needs of the other as a human being and his or her existential circumstances, untrammeled by superficial, transactional, and partisan considerations. Highlighting, prioritizing, and celebrating the best of what humanity offers with mercy and compassion, empathy and solidarity, remain the cornerstone of the exercise of his pastoral leadership. Like other hallmarks of leadership, this approach derives from a place of sincere belief in the unsullied goodness of human beings.

In the understanding of Pope Francis, by their heroic service and witness of merciful love in a time of crisis, countless women have reenacted the journey and experience of the faithful and courageous women of the gospel stories. Just as the latter braved the darkness of the night in search of the body of the crucified Lord undeterred by the danger that lay ahead, so during the pandemic have women labored courageously and selflessly on the front lines. The daring and resilience of the women of Jerusalem were rewarded with a life-changing encounter with the Risen Christ, while the women engaged in battling the scourge of the coronavirus pandemic are illuminating humanity's darkened path with compassion and mercy. The pope describes their role in combating the coronavirus pandemic as exemplary and heroic. In general, in addition to being an authentic expression of "human nature," such profound compassion and selflessness are a practical demonstration of what Francis refers to as "antibodies of solidarity," which I will discuss later in this book. In a time of crisis, celebrating goodness is anything but a philosophical or abstract exercise. Concretely, it entails identifying and highlighting that quality in the people whose actions embody and manifest it even in the most trying situations like a global public health crisis. As the pope consistently and insightfully emphasizes, these people are not always visible or celebrated. Yet their heroic acts render them indispensable to the survival of humanity, which owes its survival to their goodness, especially in a time of crisis.

Martyrs of Charity

On Holy Thursday, when the Catholic Church traditionally celebrates the institution of the priestly ministry, Pope Francis drew attention to the heavy toll COVID-19 had taken on priests. As he is wont to do, but particularly in the context of the coronavirus pandemic, he expressed his affection for and closeness to his "dear brother priests." "Today, I carry you in my heart, and I bring you to the altar."[7] In particular, Francis acknowledged many "pastor priests" who gave their lives while serving and ministering to the sick in hospitals. Like the other heroes and heroines who defied the threat of the coronavirus, they poured out their lives to bring solace to the sick and afflicted. As the pope declared in his extraordinary *Urbi et Orbi* message on March 27, 2020, they were not preoccupied with saving themselves, because they understood "that no one reaches salvation by themselves."[8]

---

[7] Pope Francis, "Holy Thursday Homily," St. Peter's Basilica, April 9, 2020 (www.vatican.va).

[8] "Extraordinary Moment of Prayer."

Particularly moving was the widely circulated, albeit disputed, story of seventy-two-year-old Italian priest Don Giuseppe Berardelli, Archpriest of Casnigo in the Diocese of Bergamo in northern Italy, one of the areas hardest hit by the coronavirus pandemic. As the story goes, stricken by COVID-19 and suffering respiratory complications, Don Berardelli made the ultimate sacrifice by giving up the use of a respirator in order to save the life of a younger coronavirus patient. This legend may be hagiographical, but it reflects the reality of people who prioritize the lives of others above theirs, especially the most vulnerable.

The liturgical lockdown during the pandemic had a particularly debilitating effect on priestly ministry. Corralled into isolated involuntary huddles like the rest of the population, many priests and religious took shelter from the tempestuous rage of COVID-19. In one sense, during the pandemic, the church bore a striking resemblance to the postresurrection community of the first disciples barricaded in the upper room—vulnerable and interconnected, yet frightful of physical proximity and of a malevolent enemy outside (see Jn 20:19). The realization that church was not meant to be catacombs for self-protection, nor was it entrapped within the four walls of a building, presented a new reality for many priests and religious during the pandemic.

Interestingly and fortuitously, the curtailing of sacramental and congregational worship has engendered a new creativity in laypeople to discover unorthodox spaces for building community and establishing connection. As Francis himself admitted, "In these months, people couldn't participate in person in liturgical celebrations, but they didn't stop feeling like a community. They prayed alone or with family, with social communications tools. They were spiritually united and aware that the embrace of the Lord extends beyond the limitations of space."[9] Examples abound of alternative ways invented to

---

[9] "Pope Thanks Italian Doctors and Health Care Workers for Heroic Service during Pandemic," *Vatican News* (www.vaticannews.va).

celebrate and minister in family and local settings such as by using relatively affordable online tools to create or follow livestreamed religious celebrations. To cite one interesting example, in Kenya some Small Christian Communities relocated to online platforms and continued to meet virtually to fulfill their mission as a new way of being "the digital Church" in the neighborhood.[10] The ability to maintain continuity amid the disruption of a pandemic further deepened these communities' sense of connection and belonging to a global community called church.

Understandably, however, the limiting effect of the liturgical lockdown posed existential questions for pastors, not least because of the expectation that personal responsibility and self-care do not override the imperative of compassionate outreach to people in need. As infection and death rates from COVID-19 soared, the challenge for pastors was to discover effective alternate ways of ministering with compassion and tenderness to those afflicted by the disease and to others confined to their homes by the necessities of social distancing. Those few who were able to minister to the sick risked infection and possibly death from the virus. In keeping with the principal points presented in this and previous chapters, by making the choice to reach out to the sick and dying, those ministers demonstrated that compassion is not a function of whether or not all is well with self; rather, it is about what is happening to the world, to others. In a time of crisis, compassion motivates the choice to become involved and affected by the predicament of the human condition and to resist the temptation of indifference. The passion and perseverance of these ministers did not go unnoticed, and should not be confused with what Francis decried as "adolescent resistance" of some ministers to public health prevention measures. In one livestreamed midday address, Francis spoke extemporaneously

---

[10] Lynn F. Monahan, "Go Digital or Die: A Maryknoll Priest Helps Small Christian Communities in Kenya Get Online during Pandemic Crisis," *Maryknoll Magazine*, June 5, 2020 (www.maryknollmagazine.org).

about their ingenuity during the crisis and thanked those pastors and people ministering in the name of the gospel who "think up a thousand ways of being close to the people, so that the people do not feel abandoned; priests with apostolic zeal that have understood well that in times of the *pandemia* one should never be one who abandons the flock." Echoes of the pope's proclivity for a pastoral model of leadership ring clearly in this heartfelt expression of gratitude.

It is in the nature of a crisis to bring out the best and the worst in human nature. People can embody either or both of these dispositions—the one to assuage pain, the other to profit from the calamity. Under such circumstances, leadership entails sincerely celebrating goodness and denouncing selfishness. The list of people who embody such goodness in a time of crisis like the coronavirus pandemic is open-ended, not exhaustive. In several instances, Pope Francis has also saluted and celebrated the courage, patience, and sacrifice of fathers, mothers, grandparents, teachers, children, cleaners, caretakers, seafarers, fishermen, police, and soldiers; and essential services like pharmacies, supermarkets, and transportation. The extent of his affinity with and affection for them is as expansive as his appreciation and gratitude are profound. Never once has Francis shown any sign of despairing in humanity's goodness.

Upon deeper reflection, the quality of celebrating goodness and recognizing the very best in people dovetails perfectly with Pope Francis's idea of sanctity and holiness as gifts of grace offered by God to all people without consideration of estate, status, class, or vocation. Goodness is a manifestation of sanctity and holiness, both of which can be found in immeasurable abundance among people in every part of the world. This is the principal theological insight that the pope elucidates in his apostolic exhortation on the call to holiness in today's world, *Gaudete et exsultate* (GE; 2018). Actually, it is by observing his formulation and articulation of the meaning of sanctity and holiness that we are able to appreciate the measure of

Pope Francis's belief in, proclamation of, and celebration of the goodness of humanity.

In his Holy Thursday Eucharist, commemorating the Last Supper of Jesus Christ before his passion and crucifixion, and during Eucharist at Casa Santa Marta on May 2, 2020, Pope Francis paid tribute to more than one hundred Italian doctors who died in the line of duty. He spoke glowingly of them as "the saints next door." At about the same time, in an interview with Austen Ivereigh, Francis provided an expanded list of "the next-door saints": "They are heroes: doctors, nurses, volunteers, religious sisters, priests, shop workers—all performing their duty so that society can continue functioning. How many doctors and nurses have died! How many religious sisters have died!"[11] He repeats the same description when he salutes nurses and midwives on International Nurses Day 2020:

> Because of your dedication, you are among the "saints next door." You are an image of the Church as a "field hospital" that continues to carry out the mission of Jesus Christ, who drew near to and healed people with all kinds of sickness and who stooped down to wash the feet of his disciples. Thank you for your service to humanity![12]

Here is the interesting fact: the pope's choice of terminology is not accidental. The expression "the saints next door" is the heading of the second part of the opening chapter of *GE*. Quite clearly, this expression provides a window into the theological underpinnings of Francis's imagination and his leadership style during the crisis of coronavirus. When he celebrates the goodness of ordinary, everyday heroes and

---

[11] Pope Francis's interview with Austen Ivereigh, "Take Care of Yourselves for a Future That Will Come," *The Tablet* (April 11, 2020), 6–8.

[12] Pope's Message for International Nurses Day, *Vatican News*, May 12, 2020 (www.vatican.va).

heroines battling COVID-19, the pope explicitly links their lives and sacrifices with a wider notion of sanctity and holiness. Whether as Christians or adherents of other faith traditions, these exemplary people are not immune to fear and apprehension in the tragic circumstances of the pandemic. Yet they are able to draw upon an interior reserve of goodness to remain courageous and generous in their self-giving.

Such goodness shines forth in a time of crisis: "Only when something happens that upsets the course of our lives do our eyes become capable of seeing the goodness of the saints 'next door,' of 'those who, living in our midst, reflect God's presence' (*GE*, 7), but without fanfare."[13] In the thinking of Pope Francis, behind their courage and generosity lies the force of the Holy Spirit who "bestows holiness in abundance among God's holy and faithful people" (*GE*, 6). Thus, for Francis, holiness is an expression of God's gift, freely given and deeply embedded in people's hearts.

The exercise of one's vocation and deployment of personal gifts and talents opens up a path that empowers and enables the emergence and radiant flourishing of "the very best of themselves." The uniqueness of each person's spiritual path precludes pretense and promotes authenticity and genuineness of witness (*GE*, 11). The multiplicity of ways of living a life of love makes it possible to bear "witness in everything we do, wherever we find ourselves" (*GE*, 14). Without discounting the paramount importance of a personal relationship with God, nurtured by a robust life of worship and prayer, as well as moral uprightness, "the ultimate criterion on which our lives will be judged is what we have done for others" (*GE*, 104). Here, of course, the reference is to the narrative of the last judgment in the chapter 25 of the Gospel of Matthew, in which people are judged according to whether or not they show acts of mercy, compassion, and care for the least of God's creation.

---

[13] "Message of Pope Francis for 2020 World Day of the Poor," 5.

This biblical criterion or standard befits many unsung heroes and heroines who have continued working in the midst of the coronavirus pandemic to ensure that essential services did not come to a complete halt and that society could continue to function with a reasonable degree of normality.

True to character, in explaining the dynamics of sanctity and holiness, Pope Francis singles out for emphasis the "genius of woman" as manifested "in feminine styles of holiness, which are an essential means of reflecting God's holiness in this world. Indeed, in times when women tended to be most ignored or overlooked, the Holy Spirit raised up saints whose attractiveness produced new spiritual vigour and important reforms in the Church" (*GE*, 12). The pope cites examples of strong, powerful, and courageous women in church history, but he does not forget "all those unknown or forgotten women who, each in her own way, sustained and transformed families and communities by the power of their witness" (*GE*, 12). We can glimpse here unmistakable resonances of his praise and celebration of women who "lit a flame of mercy" in the darkest hour of the coronavirus pandemic, giving their lives and helping and serving others. In a radical sense, the attributes of God are manifested in their dedication to the service and care of others. This, contends Francis, is holiness on display: "Seeing and acting with mercy: that is holiness" (*GE*, 82).

Given the ravages of the coronavirus pandemic, the true scale of the cost in terms of lives lost and resources exhausted in the fight against the disease will become increasingly evident, along with the open wounds and deep trauma of people impacted by the pandemic. Between the fog of memory and the dawn of hope for a world chastened by the experience of the plague, it is important not to forget or trivialize the heroic sacrifice and service of the various cadres of workers who gave their lives in order to care for and protect the lives of people around the world. Throughout his messages, reflections, and gestures, Pope Francis never ceases to celebrate these workers' goodness as "a visible sign of humanity that warms the heart."[14] The capacity to celebrate goodness in people who risk their lives to heal and defend society from the contagion of the plague serves as an index of a leader's moral fiber, authenticity, and credibility, especially in a time of crisis.

---

[14] "Pope Thanks Italian Doctors and Health Care Workers for Heroic Service during Pandemic."

4

Word and Witness

When they call to me, I will answer them; I will
be with them in trouble, I will rescue them and
honor them.

—Psalms 91:15

In a time of crisis, what means does a leader possess to communicate messages of comfort, consolation, and hope, besides
merely delivering situation updates and furnishing factual
information? A cursory review of the communication strategy
of global leaders during the coronavirus pandemic reveals a
common practice. In nearly all the cases, the preferred method
takes the form of regular briefings, updates, and news con-
ferences. In several countries across the world, coronavirus
briefings are a daily affair and widely reported. Oftentimes
such occasions become emotionally charged, politically sensi-
tive, and psychologically disconcerting. After all, a pandemic
is a matter of life and death. Fittingly, the term "bully pulpit"
gained renewed prominence to describe such events that allow
holders of public office to communicate information, propa-
gate their views, and exhort citizens to adopt certain patterns
of behavior in times of uncertainty. Not a few leaders have

used this opportunity to various influential effects, some more sanguinely than others.

The key issues covered during briefings include prevention measures, new cases of coronavirus disease, hospital admissions, availability or lack of critical equipment like ventilators and personal protective equipment, and the grim tally of fatalities. There are two observations to be made here. First, the crucial importance of effective communication derives from the nature of the crisis. In the case of the coronavirus pandemic, not only is it a matter of life and death, leaders were also confronted with a fast-moving and constantly shifting scenario with regard to all aspects of the pandemic. New information needed to be processed rapidly and appropriate responses updated accordingly. Added to that is the constant and relentless deluge of false information and fake news about the nature of the disease and its consequences. Absent a clear and consistent communication strategy, crises can morph into a fertile ground for potentially noxious information. Second, in my opinion, the macabre ritual of announcing the numbers of infections, hospitalizations, and fatalities due to COVID-19 yields mixed results. It stirs and stokes a deep yearning for the slightest thread of hope that would signal a virulent enemy in retreat. This outcome could be salutary; good, reassuring, and hopeful news is a scarce commodity in a time of crisis. However, if this basic need is handled shoddily, the resultant vacuum can be occupied quickly by an assortment of zealous fabricators of fake news and peddlers of conspiracy theories.

Unlike politicians, Pope Francis does not enjoy the opportunity and privilege of having a "bully pulpit" for daily televised briefings and updates—certainly not in the way the practice is sometimes politicized to serve partisan agendas. Yet, there is hardly a dearth of occasions and platforms for Francis to communicate his message to a global audience. From daily masses in his Casa Santa Marta residence to his twice-weekly messages from the Library of the Apostolic Palace, an iconic and well-appointed venue for receiving visiting dignitaries, the pope remains constantly in the news. During the coronavirus crisis, both religious and secular media took notice of his liturgical itinerary and pronouncements.

That is not to say that this situation was any different compared to the prepandemic period. There is never a shortage of sensational events and crises around the Vatican and the Catholic Church to pique the curiosity of the media. But in the time of COVID-19, there was a noticeable intensification of media attention to the pope's official interventions. The events at which Pope Francis presided were livestreamed, reaching millions of listeners, viewers, and followers across the globe. As already noted in the previous chapters, Francis has staged bespoke spiritual and liturgical events in response to the challenges presented by the pandemic. And the coincidence of the pandemic's outbreak with Eastertide seemed superbly propitious for the leader of the world's single largest religious community to deliver stirring, motivating, and comforting allocutions addressed to *Urbi et Orbi* (To the City and to the World).

The central thesis of this chapter holds that a balanced combination of message and medium is a valuable means for the effective exercise of leadership in a time of crisis. In previous chapters, I have examined how Pope Francis acts in his office as consoler, adopts a preference of love for the poor and vulnerable, and celebrates the inherent goodness in humanity besieged by a plague. Key to all these leadership functions or styles is the issue of communication. The main consideration is the importance of a strategically crafted practice and process of conveying messages through personable, engaging, and meaning-laden mediums. By his own admission, Francis's approach combines word and witness, the result of which is a compelling, reassuring, and transparent vision of hope in an atmosphere of crisis. Understandably, as the leader of a global community of faith, communication constitutes a key element of the pope's leadership role and function. There is nothing new here. For this function, the pope has at his disposal a wealth of time-honored resources for devising and delivering his message. A close analysis of his approach to the coronavirus pandemic offers some insightful lessons on the critical importance of communication and the mediums of communication as a constitutive dimension of good leadership during a crisis.

A Victorious Weapon

The main topic of this section is prayer. Two preliminary considerations are in order. First, in analyzing this component of Pope Francis's leadership style, it may seem odd to categorize prayer as a message and a medium of communication. The aim is not to trivialize an experience and a practice that for so many people of faith serves as a privileged moment for encountering, cultivating, and sustaining a nourishing relationship with the Ultimate Reality called God. The point that I wish to underline is how Francis uses this means to good effect in speaking and ministering to the troubled hearts of people across the globe in a time of uncertainty, fear, and anxiety, and as a remedy for their distress. Yet it is important to concede that the pope does not hold a monopoly on the use of this means. At various times, several religious and political leaders have found it a useful instrument in their repertoire of responses to the challenges posed by COVID-19. Some of these leaders were not leaders of faith communities. Naturally, for them, prayer featured only as an episodic event. On the contrary, for Pope Francis, prayer is at the heart of his response. This should not surprise us, not least because Francis is a man of faith with unquestionable mastery of the theological and spiritual realms, both in their pastoral and popular expressions. In a certain sense, his performance is akin to that of a professional within the sphere of his or her competence. Engaging with his faith community is the field where he plays best. As such, his performance is unrivaled by political leaders—just as, perhaps, Pope Francis would be considered an amateur by the latter on their turf of political intrigue and partisan maneuvering.

The second consideration is that as would be true in similar situations of crisis, the coronavirus pandemic demonstrates how much faith matters for many people. Faith is seen as a source of personal and collective comfort and reassurance amid uncertainty, confusion, and despair. A study conducted by the Pew Research Center reported that the faith of one-quarter of believing adult Christians in the US strengthened during and as a result of the coronavirus pandemic, even when most public places of worship were shuttered for many months.[1] A similar poll in the UK, commissioned by the Christian relief and development agency Tearfund, found evidence of an increase in the numbers of people turning to faith, including participation in online religious activities, during the coronavirus pandemic. Among respondents, one in twenty (5 percent) of UK adults admitted that they had started to pray during the crisis, even though they had not prayed before the pandemic. Likewise, one in five (18 percent) of UK adults said they have asked someone else to say a prayer, and one in five (19 percent) UK adults reported they have read a religious text during lockdown.[2] A wider survey of the impact of the coronavirus pandemic on UK and Irish Christians reveals that it "has led to a surge in faith," with more than half of the respondents reporting a deeper closeness to God and becoming more prayerful.[3] These findings underline a belief in the power of prayer to make a difference and bring positive change

---

[1] Claire Gecewicz, "Few Americans Say Their House of Worship Is Open, but a Quarter Say Their Faith Has Grown during Pandemic," Pew Research Center Fact Tank, April 20, 2020 (www.pewresearch.org).

[2] "Many Brits Look to Faith during Lockdown," May 30, 2020 (www.tearfund.org).

[3] Catherine Pepinster, "Catholics Brought 'Closer to God' by Covid-19," *The Tablet*, June 15, 2020 (www.thetablet.co.uk).

in a time of crisis, even for people who are not habitually faith directed. Yet this understanding of prayer needs to be carefully nuanced to avoid any misconception.

On this subject of prayer as a response to a pandemic, the experience in Africa reveals some interesting dimensions and raises some pertinent issues. There is ample evidence to suggest that some African leaders seemed particularly besotted with the use of prayer as a response to the coronavirus pandemic, at times to an unsettling degree. During the pandemic, the African religious space has generally remained vibrant and active. On a continent where religion holds sway over people's lives in ordinary and extraordinary circumstances, many people utilized an assortment of creative solutions to beat social distancing and lockdowns in order to fulfill religious obligations. For Africans of various generations and demographics, who have been stereotyped as notoriously and incurably religious, faith still mattered, even more than ever, as a powerful tool for coping with and ending personal and collective calamities. In the particular context of the coronavirus pandemic, there was hardly any shortage of religious activities and offerings. Pastors and prophets, evangelists and preachers had a field day conducting all-night prayers, anointing, prophesying, and casting and binding the evil coronavirus.

Certainly, there were many charlatans. Consider the case of Kenyan Pastor Nathan Kirimi of Jesus Winner Ministry in Meru, central Kenya, who excoriated other religious leaders who had opted to shutter their churches. Kirimi dismissed COVID-19 as a hoax fabricated to test the resolve of Christians. He ridiculed the practice of personal and public hygiene as a preventive measure. Such blatant and dangerous ignorance in a "man of God" defies belief. Here the prophetic biblical lament would seem to apply: "My people are destroyed for lack of knowledge!" (Hos 4:6). When religious leaders downplayed social distancing rules and containment measures, they exposed their members to the contagion of the virus and endangered the lives of people in their communities. Globally, there are widely attested stories of religious leaders who accelerated the spread of COVID-19 because they organized and hosted mass religious gatherings. Aside from the dubious practices of irresponsible self-styled pastors, evangelists, and prophets, many Africans—as elsewhere in the world—still sought divine intervention, egged on by religious, civil, and political authorities.

Kenya's President Uhuru Kenyatta, a practicing Catholic, was the first to decree a national day of prayer. His rationale sounded noble and compelling: "We have learnt over time that turning to God in such times gives us not only comfort but also hope and strength to overcome even those challenges that for us as humans may seem insurmountable."[4] The nation responded enthusiastically to this presidential call to prayer, which was organized, orchestrated, and streamed live from the State House by this president-turned-high priest. In Ghana, President Nana Akufo-Addo summoned Christians and Muslims to observe a national day of fasting and prayer. The intention of this national exercise was unambiguous. According to the president, "whilst we continue to adhere to these measures (social distancing, curfew, and lockdown), and ramp up our efforts to defeat this virus, I urge all of us, also, to seek the face of the Almighty. . . . Let us pray to God to protect our nation and save us from this pandemic."[5] Not to be outdone, Tanzania's President John Magufuli, another devout Catholic, declared not one but three days of national prayer "to pray to Almighty God that he deliver us from this pandemic. Let us pray each of us in their own faith. He will hear us."[6] Tanzanians duly responded to the presidential

---

[4] Hilary Kimuyu, "Uhuru Declares Saturday Day of Prayer over Coronavirus," *Nairobi News*, March 17, 2020 (www.nairobinews. nation.co.ke).

[5] Isaac Yeboah, "#Coronavirus: Ghana to Observe National Day of Fasting and Prayer," *Graphic Online,* March 22, 2020 (www.graphic. com.gh).

[6] "Covid-19: President Magufuli Urges Tanzanians to Turn to God,"

call to prayer. Appallingly, Magufuli ridiculed the practice of wearing masks and gloves and balked at the idea of banning gatherings in churches and mosques. He justified his stance with the claim that places of worship are where "there is true healing" and prayers "can vanquish" the virus. More worrisome and dubious was his assertion that "Coronavirus is a devil, it cannot live in the body of Christ, it will burn instantly. This is a time to build our faith." Quite clearly, he had strayed deep into an unfamiliar terrain, exposing his amateurish theological constructs. Magufuli would later precipitously declare Tanzania "coronavirus-free" to a jubilant and ululating congregation of worshippers: "We have been praying and fasting for God to save us from the pandemic that has afflicted our country and the world. But God has answered us. . . . The corona disease has been eliminated by God."[7] Counterintuitive and unsettling messages such as Magafuli's flew in the face of epidemiological evidence of the virulence of COVID-19 and risked further endangering the lives of Africans. The cost of the president's antics would only become evident in the steep rise of infection rates and the consequent fatalities due to COVID-19.

Clearly these performances orchestrated by politicians were episodic and sometimes opportunistic events that did not feature as core items in their job description. After all, they are not supposed to be in the business of prayer, praise, and worship. On the contrary, Pope Francis's prayerful interventions were regular, purposeful, and consistent, but not routine or casual. As we have seen, a significant part of his interventions coincided with the peak moments of Eastertide. Each moment of prayer was replete with richly evocative gestures, metaphors, and symbolisms. Not all of the moments are captured in this book. Of the moments of ritual and prayer, two were

---

The Citizen, April 17, 2020 (www.thecitizen.co.tz).

[7] "Coronavirus: John Magufuli Declares Tanzania Free of Covid-19," *The BBC*, June 8, 2020 (www.bbc.com).

visually striking and emotionally memorable—first, for their setting, namely, an empty St. Peter's Square, devoid of liturgical pomp, paraphernalia, and pageantry; and, second, the use of icons to serve as backdrop. Needless to say, these events were poignant also for their spiritual significance and effect. The two moments were the Good Friday event on April 10, 2020, and the *Urbi et Orbi* statement on March 27, 2020. I have examined some of the details of the former in the two preceding chapters, in particular chapter 2.

The Good Friday event lasted approximately ninety minutes. The central feature of the day's liturgical celebration was the Way of the Cross (*Via Crucis*). This annual event that commemorates the suffering and death of Jesus in fourteen stations is a permanent and undeletable fixture in Catholic Christian worship at Easter. However, the coronavirus pandemic forced unprecedented changes, notably the change of venue. In previous years, the popes staged the event in the dramatic and historic site of the Colosseum in Rome. The venue is famous in Roman antiquity for gladiatorial combats, games, and a controversial reputation for hosting the persecution and martyrdom of early Christians. In 2020, Pope Francis presided over the *Via Crucis* from the steps of St. Peter's Basilica. The customary teeming crowds of pilgrims, tourists, and spectators were replaced by just a handful of participants—two groups of five people, each representing health care workers and prisoners. A carefully selected list of themes, symbols, and concerns relevant to the coronavirus pandemic dominated the entire prayer event. Apart from reading prayers after each station, Francis departed from tradition and opted not to give a homily at the end of the ritual. Such was the symbolic power of this event under the circumstances of pain and agony during the coronavirus pandemic that words would have been superfluous. Yet this moment of prayer was a powerful message of hope to a suffering world, as I will explain below.

On March 27, 2020, Pope Francis led an extraordinary evening prayer service to implore divine help amid the coronavirus pandemic. In announcing the *Urbi et Orbi* event, he referred to it simply as "a moment of prayer," to which he invited people across the globe to participate virtually. On the appointed day, as the moment of prayer began, Francis shuffled across the entire length of the court of St. Peter's Square, peppered by a light drizzle as he made his way to a canopied dais. From that vantage point, alone save for one aide, the pope delivered a profoundly moving reflection to the world. The content of his reflection is interspersed across the chapters of this book. What followed his reflection bears greater importance in the perspective of this chapter.

Immediately after the outdoor service, Francis made brief stops in front of two historic and revered icons: the miraculous cross of St. Marcello Church in Rome and the image of Our Lady Salvation of the Roman People. Centuries ago, these icons played key roles in tackling public health crises in Rome. The pope then proceeded to the Basilica for a moment of quiet recollection and adoration of the Blessed Sacrament displayed in a monstrance atop an altar. His subsequent gesture was striking and moving, again for its visual effect, as well as its spiritual significance. Draped in a humoral veil, Francis proceeded to lift the monstrance from the altar. His steps were labored and his frame arched to one side as he emerged from the Basilica and approached the steps. Vividly, the octogenarian pope was struggling to bear the weight of the monstrance. Yet he bore the charge with resolve and grace. Holding the monstrance aloft on the steps of the Basilica he imparted divine benediction with the Blessed Sacrament on a world ailing from a brutal and unforgiving pestilence. Following this blessing of *Urbi et Orbi*, Francis reposed the Blessed Sacrament on the altar and departed the same way he came—alone through an empty square under a light shower of rain, as if on a pilgrimage with a world struggling to adjust and cope with its own uncertain reality at an extremely volatile moment. The pope had presided over a global moment of prayer and delivered a message of hope channeled through powerful religious symbolism in a time of crisis. His words were important, as were his gestures and chosen mediums and symbols. The use of symbolisms as props in an atmosphere of crisis even outside of a religious context bears further analysis. It is a means that leaders can use to influential effect.

Icons and Symbols of Hope

In carrying out his pastoral accompaniment and exercising his office of consolation during the pandemic, Pope Francis has used carefully selected religious icons, symbols, and metaphors to deliver his message to a global audience. As he told Spanish journalist Jordi Evole, "Today, the language of gestures is more important than words."[8] Francis's ritual gestures and actions contained potent devotional, sacramental, and pedagogical values. In part, it was the privilege and pleasure of watching him preside at events, deliver his consoling messages, and exercise his leadership role through these profoundly symbolic gestures and actions that shaped and confirmed the direction taken in the writing of this book. The genuineness of his faith, the simplicity of his delivery, and the poignancy of his message stand in sharp contrast to the hollow and shallow fabrications of some leaders.

For the Good Friday and *Urbi et Orbi* talks, two distinct religious icons framed the context of the prayer events. The first was a blackened wooden sixteenth-century crucifix from the church of St. Marcello in Via del Corso in Rome. This was no ordinary crucifix. It had seen better days—it survived a fire in 1519 and still bore the scars in the form of soot stains on the corpus. History and tradition have it that when a plague ravaged the city of Rome in 1522, devotees defied a lockdown

---

[8] Jordi Evole, "El mensaje del papa Francisco a los empresarios: 'No es momento de despedir, es momento de acoger,'" *La Vanguardia*, March 23, 2020 (www.lavanguardia.com).

and social distancing order to press the icon into service by carrying it on a sixteen-day procession to ward off the epidemic. Believers credited the cross with miraculously ending that plague. One late afternoon in March 2020, a week before the special *Urbi et Orbi* at the Vatican, Pope Francis traveled to St. Marcello on pilgrimage to this iconic crucifix. The private devotion lasted less than half an hour. It was while Francis was in prayer before this miraculous icon that he made a blunt and bold supplication: "Lord, stop it (coronavirus) with your hand!" Although sounding like a command, it was a prayer of distress issuing from the heart of a leader standing in the breach and fully conscious of the suffering and distress of countless numbers of people. As a religious leader, like the respondents to the Tearfund survey in the UK, the pope believes in the power of prayer to make a difference and to bring about positive change in the world, especially in a time of crisis.

The second image that served as an iconic prop for the special liturgical moments presided over by Pope Francis during the coronavirus pandemic was the image of a Madonna and child that is venerated as *Salus Populi Romani* (Salvation [or Health] of the Roman People). Its origins are unclear, but legends and pious myths abound about the age, material, and creator of the 3 × 5-foot painting. Some accounts sound outlandish, like the one that claims it was the handiwork of the author of Luke's Gospel, using wood from a piece of furniture crafted by Jesus of Nazareth, while Mary regaled the portraitist with extraordinary tales from her life. But like the cross of St. Marcello, this icon had a proven pedigree among Roman devotees as a trusted source of protection in times of mass affliction. As tradition goes, on two occasions—during a sixth-century plague and again during a nineteenth-century cholera outbreak—the Salvation of the Roman People played a key role in ridding the city of the epidemics. And as the name suggests, the icon was accorded the principal credit for saving the city's inhabitants. Relocated from its traditional home in the Paolina Chapel of the Basilica of St. Mary Major in Rome, it was mounted against one of the imposing columns of St. Peter's Basilica. As twice *Salus Populi Romani* offered solicitude and protection for the people of Rome in distress, the icon now offered hope and comfort for believers in search of an anchor in a time of crisis. Back in the day, the icon did not disappoint the people. One of Pope Francis's illustrious predecessors, St. Pope Gregory the Great, had borne the icon on a religious procession through the streets of Rome to plead for Mary's intercession to overcome the plague of 590 CE. Another pope, Gregory XVI, would repeat the salutary ritual in 1837 for the same cause of invoking Mary's aid to end a cholera epidemic. Pope Pius XII made a pilgrimage to the icon in June 1944 to pray for the deliverance of the city of Rome as Nazi troops retreated from Italy during World War II. The parallels of these historical moments with the crisis of the coronavirus are as unmistakable as the icon's reputation in a time of crisis is uncontestable—at least for devotees like Francis.

Besides the symbol-laden history of the Madonna's image, for Pope Francis the icon carries a personal significance. Francis is a regular visitor to *Salus Populi Romani*. Since his first visit to the icon on the morning of his election as pope in March 2013, he has made a religious duty of visiting it before and after every international trip. Considering that his international apostolic visits include thirty-two trips to no fewer than fifty countries in seven years, Francis is a familiar and recognizable guest of the Madonna and child. As the storm of the coronavirus gathered momentum, Pope Francis paid a special visit to the icon in the afternoon of March 15, 2020. The setting for this visit amplified the momentous situation of the world and enveloped it in an aura of a religious pilgrimage rather than a casual devotional pit stop. The pope laboriously navigated a narrow uphill alley leading to the church, emptied of passers-by by the Italian government's containment measures of lockdown and social distancing. On the testimony of the director of the Holy See Press Office, Matteo Bruni, the pope's intentions during his private pilgrimage to these icons were dictated entirely by the affliction unleashed on the world by the coronavirus pandemic. As he did in St. Marcello before the miraculous crucifix, Francis beseeched the intercession of *Salus Populi Romani,* who participated in Jesus's pain at the foot of the Cross with steadfast faith, "to rid the world of the pandemic. He prayed also for the healing of the many sick people struck by the virus, and for the numerous victims, and their families and friends. He prayed too for the health workers, the doctors, nurses, volunteers and those working to guarantee the smooth functioning of the society."[9] Here, as he did in St. Marcello, Pope Francis left a votive offering of a bouquet of roses in front of *Salus Populi Romani* in the Basilica of St. Mary Major. His act of devotion did not end there. He also composed and shared two new prayers to implore the help of the Virgin Mary during the coronavirus pandemic to bring an end to this great suffering and trial and to usher in a new dawn of hope, healing, and peace.

One could argue that these icons were auspiciously suited to devotional and sacramental practice in the time of a pandemic. Their significance, though, can be seen through a wider optic. When these icons were utilized by Pope Francis in his preparation for the moments of prayer and supplications at St. Peter's Basilica during Holy Week and Easter, their import rested not only on their devotional value, but primarily on their symbolic efficacy in communicating a reassuring message to the city of Rome and to the whole world in distress. This attests to the potency of faith and hope. In the turmoil of the coronavirus pandemic, when fear, confusion, and anxiety tested the faith of many, Pope Francis

---

[9] Gerard O'Connell, "Pope Francis Prays in Rome Churches Asking God to Rid the World of the Coronavirus," *America*, March 15, 2020 (www.americamagazine.org).

mobilized the rich resources of religion to appeal to people across a wide religious spectrum, in order to offer the world a medium for renewing and reposing faith in God who alone heals, protects, and redeems a broken humanity. As a religious leader, prayer and symbolism are means that he deftly deploys to beneficial effect.

I Asked the Lord to Stop the Epidemic

In William Shakespeare's *The Life and Death of Julius Caesar*, one of the principal characters, Marcus Brutus, musing about his role in the rapidly unfolding political intrigues of the day, declares, "It is the bright day that brings forth the adder." In many ways, as I hinted at the beginning of this chapter, the coronavirus pandemic has also brought out the worst in religion. Self-styled prophets, pastors, preachers, and evangelists have proposed fake cures and dubious remedies. Others have claimed to have extraordinary powers to stop the virus. There is a story that has been widely circulated on social media about a preacher from Nigeria's Glorious Mount of Possibility Church who vowed to travel to Wuhan, China, to destroy the coronavirus at its source. As fate would have it, so the story goes, the China-bound quixotic preacher ended up in an intensive care unit of a local hospital stricken by the virus that he had set out to extinguish. The first part of the story is true, but the second part is fake news; its fabricator(s) used the photo of an unrelated patient hospitalized in a Lagos hospital in 2017.

Another example of a pathological religious performance in the time of a global health crisis concerns a megapastor, Nigerian Chris Oyakhilome, who was sanctioned by the UK's communication regulatory authority for repeating a spurious claim on TV that linked the source of COVID-19 with 5G phone networks and—like the rogue former Vatican diplomat, Archbishop Carlo Maria Viganò—alleging a sinister plot to create a new anti-Christian world order. He was one of many such peddlers of fake news and conspiracy theories. Even more troubling was the case of London-based Kenyan head preacher of The Kingdom Church, Bishop Climate Wiseman, who came under investigation by the UK's Charities Commission for selling so-called COVID-19 protection kits. The kits consist of a bottle of oil and some red yarn. The pastor claimed that his followers could only be protected and saved by faith, as was the case during outbreaks of plagues in biblical times. He instructed them to anoint themselves with the divine anti-plague protection oil and wear the scarlet yarn on their bodies. Wiseman was already well established in the trade of retailing unproven spiritual remedies. Besides the plague protection kits, the preacher regularly offers anointing oils for an assortment of problems, including oils for peace, unlimited success, and good marriages. Such a degree of exploitation and trivialization of religion is unsettling. In a time of high anxiety, when people face the ambiguous threat of a deadly virus, religion is one of many tools that scammers employ to profit from people's fears. According to Wiseman, the active ingredients in his protection oil are "cedar wood, hyssop, and prayer."

To stay with the third of the bishop's ingredients, I have examined the role of prayer in Pope Francis's response to the coronavirus pandemic. Far from being exploitative, Francis has engaged in prayer as a means of fortifying faith, dispensing hope, and spreading charity. He specifically called prayer a "victorious weapon," without suggesting that it offers an antidote in the way that some pastors, preachers, and prophets have advertised their spiritual wares. When Pope Francis was queried by Italian journalist Paolo Rodari about his prayer intention on his solitary pilgrimages to the Basilica of Saint Mary Major and the church of St. Marcello, he did not mince words: "I asked the Lord to stop the epidemic. Lord, stop it with your hand. That is what I prayed."[10] The authoritative

---

[10] Paolo Rodari, "Pope Francis on Coronavirus Crisis: 'Don't Waste These Difficult Days. While at Home Re-Discover the Importance of

tone of this extremely straightforward petition laced with a hint of defiance may appear to some people as hubris. Traditionally, prayer is understood as the raising of one's mind and heart to God. The requisite attitude and posture are suppliant, humble, and self-effacing. The gospel vignette of the self-conceited Pharisee and the repentant publican comes to mind as a lesson against arrogance, condescension, and self-assurance in addressing supplications to God (see Lk 18:9–14). But by nature, Francis is neither snobbish nor arrogant. In the dark and trying times of the coronavirus pandemic, he has maintained an attitude of prayer, equanimity, and recollection that is edifying for its profundity and comforting for its simplicity. Only from a deep conviction of faith and hopeful audacity could such a self-assured statement have emerged, uttered by a person for whom "prayer and quiet service are our victorious weapons"; prayer is "the breath of faith, a cry arising from the hearts of those who trust in God."[11]

In addition to what we have seen in previous chapters, the intentions of Francis's prayers, intercessions, and supplications during the adversity of coronavirus have been varied to meet the needs of the moment. Also, at every Eucharist at which Francis has presided, he has focused his attention on a category or group of people affected by the coronavirus pandemic: expectant mothers, undertakers, teachers, students, artists, families closed up in their homes, victims of domestic violence, men and women who work in the media, the Red Cross and Red Crescent organizations, trash collectors, street cleaners, etc. This inclusiveness was further demonstrated when Pope Francis led a global recitation of the rosary to invoke the aid of the Virgin Mary amid the pandemic. Those who led parts of the prayer represented various categories of people particularly affected by the coronavirus, namely,

---

Hugging Kids and Relatives,'" *La Repubblica,* March 18, 2020 (www.repubblica.it).

[11] Pope Francis, General Audience, May 6, 2020.

a doctor and a nurse, for all the health staff committed on the front line in hospitals; a healed person and one who lost a family member, for all those touched personally by the coronavirus; a priest, hospital chaplain, and a Sister nurse, for all priests and consecrated persons close to all those tried by the disease; a pharmacist and a journalist, for all the people that even in the period of the pandemic have continued to carry out their service in favour of others; a volunteer of Civil Protection with his family, for those that have done their utmost to address this emergency and for all the vast world of volunteers; and a young family, to whom a baby was born in this period, sign of hope and of victory of life over death.[12]

The symbolic value of this spiritual choreography is unmistakable.

Besides the focus on individual persons and needs, another striking aspect of Francis's use of prayer is his singular ability to focus on the consequential challenges of the moment. His moments of prayer always capture key concerns, as his prayer during the May 24 Regina Caeli address clearly demonstrates:

Loving God, Creator of Heaven, of earth and of all that they contain. Open our minds and touch our hearts, so that we can be part of Creation, your gift. Be present to the needy in these difficult times, especially the poorest and most vulnerable. Help us to show creative solidarity in addressing the consequences of this global pandemic. Make us courageous in embracing the changes geared to the search for the common good. Now more than ever, may we be able to feel that we are all interconnected and interdependent. Make sure that we succeed in listening and responding to the cry of the earth

---

[12] "A Statement by the Pontifical Council for Promoting the New Evangelization" (May 26, 2020).

and to the cry of the poor. May the present sufferings be the birth pangs of a more fraternal and sustainable world.[13]

Besides focusing on consequential matters, a distinct thread that runs through these devotional and spiritual moments is the expression of closeness, care, and compassion for women and men, communities and countries, impacted by the pandemic. Francis's indulgence in prayer resembles anything but a religious exhibitionism or opportunism. Above all else, it is a manifestation of his office of consolation, preference of love for the poor and vulnerable, and celebration of goodness of humanity. Together these are hallmarks of leadership in a time of crisis.

It is possible to recall many moments of prayer and dramatic gestures of faith provided and presided over by Pope Francis since the outbreak of the coronavirus pandemic. However, for Francis, *prayer* in its varied expressions and forms cannot be dissociated from *witness* embodied in ritual actions and concrete gestures of compassion and solidarity. Together with those highlighted above, each moment conveys a message anchored in and channeled through symbolic mediums that heighten their perceived significance and efficacy. Amid the crisis, Francis has borne the weight of a momentous religious tradition rooted in the power of prayer and sustained by an unflinching trust in God's desire to save and protect humanity from the pandemic. The frequently recurring metaphors in his reflection on the coronavirus pandemic include storm, desert, silence, and darkness, all of which possess the capacity to severely weaken faith, dissipate hope, and threaten human certainties. At such moments and in previous centuries, pandemics have been occasions for shared supplications for divine intervention. In my opinion, the pope has provided the most widely viewed, visible, and valued demonstration of spiritual

---

[13] Pope Francis, Regina Caeli Address, May 24, 2020 (www.vatican.va).

leadership, by guiding the global community on its journey in search of solace and to rediscover a sense of peace in a time of crisis. At a time when many people of faith or no faith at all experienced a turbulent storm that roused one of the most intractable and existential questions of our time—"Where is God?"—Pope Francis took his place on the world stage in a moment of prayer. From "this colonnade that embraces Rome and the whole world," he led the global community to rekindle faith and allay its fears: "Do not be afraid. . . . We have an anchor: by his cross, we have been saved. We have a rudder: by his cross, we have been redeemed. We have hope: by his cross, we have been healed and embraced so that nothing and no one can separate us from God's redeeming love."

5

Building Bridges

I have other sheep that do not belong to this fold.
I must bring them also, and they will listen to my
voice. So there will be one flock, one shepherd.

—*John 10:16*

One of the several official Latin epithets bestowed on popes is *Pontifex Maximus*. It translates literally as "Greatest Bridge-builder." Unsurprisingly, it is not a title that Pope Francis is wont to append to his papal missives and encyclicals. His reticence may not be out of discontent or disdain for its meaning but due to Francis's characteristic aversion for the pomp and paraphernalia of papal nomenclature and office. That being said, @Pontifex is the Twitter handle of the official Twitter page of Pope Francis, counting over eighteen million followers. Even the more prestigious and venerable title *Vicarius Christi* (Vicar of Christ) has not succeeded in tempting his fancy. Here again, the reluctance might testify to something else. The pope understands that these appellations are not value neutral, and he understands the limit of his powers and the weight of theological contention around the conception and exercise of papal authority in Christian tradition and history. So instead he has settled for the somewhat bland but more accurate tag *Vescovo di Roma* (Bishop of Rome). Yet, bridge-building is a task that Francis seems to excel at as a core component of his leadership style.

In concrete terms, building a bridge requires precise skills in conception, design, and construction. Whether it is a sophisticated engineering feat or a ramshackle, makeshift structure, a bridge is primarily utilitarian. A universal wisdom prescribes that a bridge ought to serve a clear purpose and function. It should lead somewhere rather than nowhere. Some bridges, though, carry a symbolic value for their history, design, and aesthetic appeal. In times of conflict, bridges are prized trophies for militants to disrupt supply lines, frustrate the enemy's advance, or secure strategic routes. There are many stories about bridges, some of them told through the medium of film and cinema. My all-time favorites are David Lean's *The Bridge on the River Kwai* and Clint Eastwood's *The Bridges of Madison County*. Songs have been written about bridges as well. I think of "Bridge over Troubled Water" by Simon and Garfunkel. As a child in primary school, I remember hearing a song popular among children with the lyrics "London Bridge is falling down, falling down, falling down." Never having seen one in my childhood, I hadn't the faintest idea what London Bridge looked like, or why anybody, not least children in a faraway city, should care about its collapse. Still children sang.

In his book *The Liminal Papacy of Pope Francis*, Massimo Faggioli executes a superb analysis of the geographical and historical import of the title *Pontifex* as a programmatic revelation of the theological vision of liminality and direction of Pope Francis's pontificate. Like other papal titles, it is loaded with meaning, employed with intent, and shaped by centuries of tradition. The intention of this chapter is not to engage in an intellectual debate about theological claims and counterclaims regarding the understanding of the pope's authority and the powers reflected in official titles. The aim is to show how Francis exercises the role of a bridge-builder in the context of a global public health crisis without wearing the title on his proverbial sleeve. Whether Francis admits it or not, experience strongly validates his role as a builder of bridges. A careful study of his words, messages, and gestures in the time of the coronavirus pandemic reveals the critical importance of the art and skill of bridging all manner of divides in search of common ground at a time of crisis. Francis exemplifies this art and skill in many ways. Given the rich connotations and historical pedigree of this reality, I find bridge-building a useful metaphor for conceptualizing and understanding how Francis leads in the time of a global health pandemic. This aspect of Francis's leadership builds on and complements previously discussed aspects of leadership in a time of crisis.

Convener in Chief

When Jesus of Nazareth cast himself in the image of a shepherd in the tenth chapter of the Johannine gospel, he signaled that the task of gathering and leading the flock thrives more on credibility than on ability. Credibility serves as a reliable criterion for clearly discerning what good leadership looks like. The good, true, and self-sacrificing shepherd exemplifies the primacy of credibility in leadership. On the contrary, the hireling, impostor, and plunderer rely on brute force and guile. Perhaps sheep are not the stupid and clueless animals that they are sometimes portrayed to be. Just the opposite. They know the good shepherd; they hear and recognize his or her voice, and they listen. This pastoralist model is akin to the function of convening. Francis accords priority to this model of leadership.[1] A caveat: Evocative as this biblical imagery may seem, it should be stripped of any conception that surreptitiously depicts communities of believers as docile and infantile while allowing their leaders to arrogate to themselves an aura of superiority and

---

[1] See Archbishop Justin Welby, "Sheep," in *A Pope Francis Lexicon*, ed. Joshua J. McElwee and Cindy Wooden (Collegeville, MN: Liturgical Press, 2018), 178–80.

authoritarian license as "enlightened" guides. My use of this imagery does not endorse a monopoly of knowledge, enlightenment, or privilege as the exclusive preserve of leaders.

Like a true shepherd, when Pope Francis has proposed or convened global religious and spiritual initiatives, the response has been wholehearted and positive. One such effort occurred when he convened a worldwide audience to participate in a moment of shared global prayer on March 25, 2020. The idea was as simple as the impact remarkable. Francis invited heads of the churches and leaders of all the Christian communities, and believers of various confessions and traditions across the globe to join in the contemporaneous and unanimous recitation of the Lord's Prayer to implore God's mercy for humanity sorely afflicted by the coronavirus. The methodology was uncomplicated—as the pope explained: "We will do so together, Christians of every church and community, of every age, language and nations."[2] The coalition of willing participants underscored the pope's appeal as a credible convener. They included Orthodox, Anglican, and Protestant church leaders who encouraged their worldwide communities to participate wholeheartedly from wherever they could. At the same time, parallel prayer events happened among Jewish communities and Muslim communities across the world. At the behest of Pope Francis, these communities united their voices around a common intention to beseech God to deliver the world from the clutches of the plague.

In this same spirit, Francis endorsed and participated in an interfaith day of prayer on May 14, 2020. The event was organized for believers of all religions and of different traditions, to unite spiritually to pray, fast, and implore God to help humanity overcome the coronavirus pandemic and many other pandemics assailing the world's poor and marginalized populations. The background of this initiative bears the imprint of

---

[2] Cindy Wooden, "Pope, Christian Leaders around the Globe Join in Prayer for Pandemic's End," *Crux*, March 25, 2020 (www.cruxnow.com).

Francis's leadership. The idea of a global day of prayer came from the Higher Committee for Human Fraternity, a group that originated from Pope Francis's historic trip to the United Arab Emirates in February 2019. On that occasion, the pope signed an interfaith "Document on Human Fraternity for World Peace and Living Together," jointly with Sheikh Ahmed el-Tayeb, the Grand Imam of Islam's leading religious center, the Al Azhar Mosque and University. The convocation of interfaith events is sometimes fraught with tension and contention. Against a tendency to consider such initiatives as a form of "religious relativism," Francis counters that they create the conditions for bridging division and enhancing interfaith unity in the face of a common threat. In his understanding,

> We are not praying against one another, this religious tradition against that other, no! We are all united as human beings, as brothers and sisters, praying to God according to our own culture, according to our own tradition, according to our own beliefs, but as brothers and sisters praying to God and this is important![3]

What Francis did at a global level during the pandemic, he also did at a national level. One example is when he led the national recitation of the rosary in Italy to invoke the intercession of St. Joseph on his feast day (March 19) for the protection of Italy, Europe, and the world. Also, at his General Audience on the feast day (April 29) of St. Catherine of Siena (1347–80), Francis invoked her intercession for the same intention: "I ask Saint Catherine to protect Italy during this pandemic; and to protect Europe, because she is a Patroness of Europe; may she protect the whole of Europe, so that it remains united."[4]

---

[3] Courtney Mares, "Pope Francis Calls People of All Religions to Pray for End of Pandemic," *Catholic News Agency*, May 14, 2020 (www.catholicnewsagency.com).

[4] Pope Francis, General Audience, April 29, 2020 (www.vatican.va).

Whether at a global or national level, Pope Francis understands such moments of collective prayer as "a sign of unity" of all people in a time of crisis. He explained his position to *La Repubblica's* Paolo Rodari. In the midst of crisis, hope is not a monopoly of people of faith; it is a common good, in which people who do not profess any faith explicitly have an equal stake:

> They are all God's children and are looked upon by him. Even those who have not yet met God, those who do not have the gift of faith, can find their way through this, in the good things they believe in: They can find strength in love for their children, for their family, for their brothers and sisters.[5]

In the context of Francis's role as a global religious leader, the convocation for collective rituals serves as a uniting factor in a time of crisis. The pope's prayer moments or events are hardly ever local. They are almost always global. Only a leader with the caliber, credibility, and global reach of Francis could stage international moments of prayer to such beneficial effects. Yet it is not a completely unattainable feat for other leaders in their local contexts, given the right disposition and conditions.

Outside of convening for religious and spiritual purposes, another key dimension of the bridge-building vocation of Pope Francis derives from his ability to reach out and to authentically engage with others beyond the boundaries of his religious and confessional constituency.[6] Here his focus is on political,

---

[5] Paolo Rodari, "Pope Francis on Coronavirus Crisis: 'Don't Waste These Difficult Days. While at Home Re-Discover the Importance of Hugging Kids and Relatives,'" *La Repubblica*, March 18, 2020 (www.repubblica.it).

[6] Faggioli provides a comprehensive account of Francis's "bridge-building geopolitics" in the context of globalization in *The Liminal Papacy of Pope Francis: Moving toward Global Catholicity* (Maryknoll, NY: Orbis Books, 2020), 155–79.

secular, and civil society leaders and authorities. Consider the case of Europe, where the coronavirus pandemic has hit particularly hard; countries like Italy, Spain, France, and the UK took turns in leading the chart of infection rates and fatalities. Also, the pandemic left the economy of major European countries in ruins. The grim situation roiled nations and shook the European Union to its foundation, even threatening its disintegration. Although uninvited, Francis stepped into the breach to offer a voice of reason, calm, and consideration. His insightful analysis of the crisis facing Europe found a positive reception among leaders in Europe. In the pope's estimation, Europe was facing "an epochal challenge" that could potentially cast the European project asunder and have a momentous repercussion for the entire world. Pope Francis ventured a solution. He counseled renewed solidarity and dialogue in the spirit of the "fraternal unity dreamt of by the founding fathers of the European Union." His message resonated with many leaders and people across the twenty-seven member nations of the Union. Furthermore, in exercising this role as convener, Francis has frequently coordinated his interventions with other leaders. He joined UN Secretar-General António Guterres—and later the UN Security Council—to call for an immediate cessation of armed hostilities in all parts of the world in order to create humanitarian corridors to deliver aid to people in coronavirus-hit conflict zones. Also, the pope reached out to and engaged with global thought leaders, such as when he penned a letter to the president of the Pan-American Committee of Men and Women Judges for Social Rights, Roberto Andrés Gallardo, on the priorities of governments in the time of a pandemic and their implications for human rights.

In chapter 1, we saw how Pope Francis exercises the ministry of consolation for people in distress. While his office of consolation shows a preference of love for the poor and vulnerable, as we saw in chapter 2, Francis does not exclude those entrusted with the responsibility of political and economic leadership. This category includes heads of state and governments as well as mayors, governors, legislators, and business leaders, whom the pope refers to as "men and women who have a political vocation." His methodology of engagement is a holistic approach that aims to prioritize the needs of the weakest members of society but without excluding others, especially people with a particular responsibility to determine the direction of society. On them reposes the duty to make a difference and create conditions that are conducive to human flourishing. This approach represents a creative combination of strategic intent and prophetic engagement, as I will show below.

Francis displays a remarkable sensitivity to people with political responsibility and an appreciation for their situation in moments of crisis. Praying for them at the Eucharist in Casa Santa Marta on May 2, 2020, he implored God to "help them and give them strength because their work is not easy." He explained that, oftentimes, in the heat of crisis, their decisions are unpopular, albeit intended largely for the good of their people. As a result, they feel isolated and misunderstood. This attention to the needs of political leaders evidences the leadership style of a pope whose primary aim is to unite and gather rather than exclude and divide people. It is yet another aspect of the exercise of the office of consolation, a preference of love, and a consciousness of the goodness of humanity, notwithstanding personal failings and limitations. Interestingly, it is not inconceivable that Pope Francis's sympathy for people with the vocation of political leadership is a cathartic reflection of his own experience of the challenges of leadership. Examples of these challenges abound in some recent publications about his pontificate that tend to focus on the resistance and opposition to Francis's various reform initiatives in the Catholic Church. Austen Ivereigh, for example, has explored incisively Francis's fraught attempt to transform the Catholic Church, as have Christopher Lamb and Massimo Faggioli. Whether or not the pope is seeing a reflection of his own struggle in the monumental challenges facing political leaders of the day in a time of crisis, his sensitivity to their situation and manner of engagement with them betrays no trace of tension or hint of turmoil. Accordingly, for political and business leaders, Francis has adopted the approach of accompaniment, intercession, and prayers, in order that they be granted wisdom to fulfill their duties and responsibilities in favor of the common good. As the pope declared in his Regina Caeli address on May 24, 2020, his care for them translates into a prayer

> for all persons of goodwill that, in this difficult time, work in every part of the world with passion and commitment for peace, for dialogue between nations, for service to the poor and for the protection of Creation and humanity's victory over any disease of body, of heart and of soul.[7]

More concretely, consider one example of the pope's positive engagement with people who have a political vocation. Not for the first time, on April 21, 2020, Pope Francis took a phone call from President Emmanuel Macron of France. At the time of the call, France, like the rest of Europe, was reeling from the devastating consequences of the pandemic. Whatever the agenda of the caller, the occasion presented an opportunity for Francis to express his solidarity and closeness to the people of France in a time of distress and support for the effort of the president to combat the virus. A formal statement from the French government confirmed that their views also converged around global issues such as debt reduction and forgiveness for poorer countries and the cessation of armed conflicts, terrorism, and hostilities. On May 4, 2020, Pope Francis would conduct a similar exchange with President Macky Sall of Senegal, a predominantly Muslim country in West Africa. On the same day, following the conversation, Sall tweeted that he endorsed Francis's response to the COVID-19

---

[7] Pope Francis, Regina Caeli Address, May 24, 2020 (www.vatican.va).

crisis: "I welcome our convergence of views on the cancellation of debt and his response to the pandemic through his call
for the universality of prayer, fraternity, and solidarity."[8] These
two examples may not be the only time that Francis chose
to reach out to political leaders during the coronavirus crisis.
No matter the frequency of outreach, the important lesson to
retain is the dimension of his leadership as a credible convener.
This quality is manifested in a variety of ways, notably, in this
instance, by reaching out to political leaders to offer support
and encouragement in the fulfillment of their duties. It also
serves as an example of what Francis describes as a "quiet
service" on behalf of humanity in distress.

The idea of convening merits further analysis to better situate it as a critical leadership function in a time of crisis. In
all the foregoing occasions revealing the quiet service of Pope
Francis as *Pontifex*, there exists a subtext that uniquely stands
him in good stead, namely, his extraordinary power to convene.
As I pointed out in the introduction, the pope's "power" contrasts sharply with the use of brute force to police and impose
lockdowns, confinement, and social distancing during the
coronavirus pandemic. Francis is anything but a "strongman."[9]
Vaticanologist John L. Allen Jr. has offered arguably the most
cogent and compelling account of this unique characteristic of
the pope's leadership role as a bridge-builder. As Allen explains
it, the pope's power to convene or his "magnetic attraction"
does not rely on political calculations or coercion.[10] Evidently,
he is not elected to office by the will and consent of a popular
majority to which he is beholden. Nor does he need to produce
a manifesto of policies, promises, and programs to ingratiate

---

[8] Magdalene Kahiu, "Senegal's President Recounts His 'Constructive Conversation with Pope Francis,'" *aciafrica,* May 6, 2020 (www.
aciafrica.org).

[9] Faggioli, *The Liminal Papacy of Pope Francis,* 172.

[10] John L. Allen Jr., "Child Safety Summit Reflects Pope's 'Extraordinary' Power to Convene," *Crux,* October 4, 2017 (www.cruxnow.com).

himself with an electorate. There are those analysts and commentators who would have us believe that politics is the key determinant in papal elections and business, and that Francis's pontificate is no exception. Be that as it may. In regard to the power to convene, the fundamental key is the pope's moral authority, which offers him a credible platform to advance and engage in issues that he considers as priorities for action. Consequently, it is rarely the case that anybody would turn down an invitation from the pope. On the contrary, his company is highly respected and coveted by leading figures for a variety of reasons and mixed motives. Regardless, it counts as a political asset that various popes have used to varying degrees of success in contemporary times.

Furthermore, the pope's power to convene reflects a form of soft power that is neither coercive nor aggressive, but is persuasive, attractive, and constructive on the basis of the credibility of his moral authority and personal integrity. The conception, deployment, and timing of this soft power is a reliable indicator of what the pope considers to be priorities not only for the church but also for the world. As such, when viewed through the prism of priorities for action, convening contains a strategic intent. There is a clear end that regulates the use of this political asset. As Allen explains, "Perhaps everybody would say yes to an invite from the pope, but the pope can't actually invite everybody—they have to pick and choose, depending on perceived degrees of urgency and importance."[11] Observing Pope Francis's messages and activities during the coronavirus pandemic, there is an unmistakable consistency in his articulation of the matters that he considers urgent and important. One clear example is his emphasis on the ethical principle of the common good, and why the needs and necessities of people and communities are paramount and should not be subjected to or subverted by the economic gains and political interests of the few, powerful, and

---

[11] Ibid.

privileged. Francis's salubrious view of the common good and his repeated insistence on it in his messaging during the coronavirus crisis demonstrate a strategic, ethical, and purposeful deployment of soft power, which reflects the pope's extraordinary power to convene.

For a balanced account, it is important to note the fact that the relationship between church and state has not been devoid of tension during the coronavirus crisis. One example comes to mind. After several weeks of strict lockdown, when the government of Italy introduced a phased easing of restrictions and permitted the reopening of some businesses and the freedom of movement for home-bound citizens, it maintained its prohibition of religious worship, like masses and weddings. Churches had to wait a few more weeks for the resumption of liturgical celebrations with the physical presence of worshippers. The Italian government's decision elicited a strong reaction from the Italian Episcopal Conference. In the estimation of the latter, the move amounted to a compromise of religious freedom. Also, the bishops accused the government of utter disregard for the essential services rendered by clergy, religious personnel, and the Catholic Church to help and support the poor and vulnerable Italians. Besides, as the bishops argued, the church's commitment to serve the poor and vulnerable during a public health emergency is rooted in a life of faith that thrives on religious and sacramental activities. Essentially, they perceived an overreach of the government's responsibility for ensuring public health and safety, in relation to the autonomy of the church in organizing the life of its faith communities. In neighboring France, the bishops reacted in a similar fashion when the government decided to delay the resumption of public worship. Ironically, in a country renowned for its fierce adherence to the principle of *laicité* or secularism, the French courts sided with religious communities and ruled against the government's ban on gatherings for public worship. Tension between church and state is not unusual, but it can be amplified in a time of crisis, as these examples demonstrate.

An Eyewitness Account

The author of Luke's Gospel opens the narrative by taking note of previous efforts by many to "set down an orderly account of the events that have been fulfilled among us, just as they were handed on to us by those who from the beginning were eyewitnesses" (Lk 1:1–2). Without claiming to be an eyewitness, the evangelist explains the methodology and purpose of the gospel account, namely, "after investigating everything carefully from the very first, to write an orderly account for you, most excellent Theophilus, so that you may know the truth concerning the things about which you have been instructed" (1:3–4). In like manner, everything written in this book is based on an accurate observation and investigation to the extent possible. This section, however, is an eyewitness account of Pope Francis's deployment of his extraordinary soft power to convene an event of consequential political implications that I was privileged to facilitate and participate in.[12]

On April 11, 2019, the world witnessed an event of extraordinary significance. It was a spiritual retreat organized for the factions in South Sudan's protracted war of attrition. The event was portrayed as a time of grace dedicated to reflection and prayer, and to ask God for a future of peace and prosperity for the people of South Sudan. As Africa's youngest independent nation, South Sudan has rarely enjoyed a moment of peace for its population of 12 million people, many of whom are impoverished and forcibly displaced within and across its borders, and with approximately 400,000 killed. The venue of the spiritual retreat was Pope Francis's residence and guesthouse, Casa Santa Marta, in the Vatican. In attendance were the two protagonists, President Salva Kiir Mayardit and opposition leader and arch-enemy Riek Machar, plus a select group of political allies. They were joined by the leaders of the

---

[12] See Giada Aquilino, "Spiritual Retreat with South Sudan Leaders in Vatican: Time to Choose Life," *Vatican News*, April 11, 2020 (www.vaticannews.va).

country's eight major churches under the auspices of the Council of Churches of South Sudan.

The spiritual, ecumenical, and diplomatic event was the brilliant initiative of the Archbishop of Canterbury and Primate of the Anglican Community, the Reverend Justin Welby, working with the Very Reverend John Chalmers, former moderator of the Presbyterian Church of Scotland. Strikingly, Pope Francis issued personal invitations to the participants and hosted the retreat. As Allen points out in his discussion of the pope's extraordinary power to convene, "virtually nobody can say no to an invitation from the pope."[13] Not a single invitee declined the pope's invitation, a rare feat that even the continental body, the African Union, would have found daunting, if not impossible.

Although Pope Francis was the chief host of the historic event, he had only a minor role assigned to him during the retreat. He was scheduled to give the closing remarks and distribute copies of the Bible to the participants as a symbol of peace. Unbeknownst to all, Francis had prepared a unique symbol of his own. His exhortation was profoundly moving, and he concluded it with an emotional appeal to Kiir and Machar:

> I ask, as a brother: remain in peace. I ask you this wholeheartedly. Let us go forward. There will be many problems, but do not be fearful, go forward, solve the problems. You have begun a process: may it finish well. There will be disagreements between you both, yes. These also should remain in the office, but before the people, hands united. In this way, as ordinary citizens you will become Fathers of the Nation. Allow me to ask you this from the heart and with my deepest sentiments.[14]

---

[13] Allen, "Child Safety Summit Reflects Pope's 'Extraordinary' Power to Convene."

[14] Address of His Holiness Pope Francis, "Spiritual Retreat for Civil and Ecclesiastical Authorities of South Sudan," April 11, 2019 (www.vatican.va).

To convey his message personally to his addressees, assisted by an aide, Francis walked toward the warlords and with great difficulty knelt down and kissed the feet of each one of the stunned leaders. It was an extraordinary symbolic gesture performed in the full glare of the global media.

The pope's dramatic gesture has been interpreted in a variety of ways. To understand its deep significance, we need to go back to the traditions and cultures of Africa. In many African cultures, age is respected. The celebrated Nigerian author, Chinua Achebe, wrote in his classic novel, *Things Fall Apart*, "Age was respected among his people, but achievement was revered." As the embodiment of wisdom, elders enjoy close proximity to the gods and ancestors. Their mode of communication is often steeped in symbolisms and metaphorical gestures. When an African parent or elder kneels in front of a younger person to make a request or a plea, the latter knows that he or she is morally obliged to acquiesce. A more dramatic gesture is when a parent or an elder disrobes to make a request or plead in front of a younger person. To refuse to honor the wishes of an elder, accompanied by such a gesture of abasement, is to risk incurring the wrath of the gods and the ancestors. The South Sudanese who participated in the spiritual retreat are all Christians. Primarily, though, they are Africans and each one of them would be familiar with the critical importance of gestures such as that of Pope Francis. If the spiritual retreat contributed anything to the peace process in South Sudan, it would be significantly because of the compelling nature of Francis's symbolic gesture and his unprecedented convening of belligerent leaders to participate jointly in a spiritual event. The leaders responsible for the conflict in South Sudan would be aware that they could not ignore the wishes of an elderly pope kneeling in front of them to kiss their feet. The consequences could be grave. In religious traditions, kneeling is a suppliant gesture, but, in the context of African reverence for age and seniority, it takes on a deeper meaning.

Francis's gesture embodied a confluence of religious and cultural symbolisms, word and witness, strategically deployed to create a path toward reconciliation, justice, and peace in a troubled nation. Remarkably, on February 22, 2020, former South Sudanese rebel leader Riek Machar was sworn in as the nation's first vice president, initiating a halting peace deal aimed at ending years of civil war. Only a leader with the credibility and moral authority of Pope Francis could have brought these battle-hardened sworn enemies to pray together in the same room and fulfill the supplication to God in the Roman Catholic "Eucharistic Prayer for Reconciliation"—to change human hearts to prepare them for reconciliation so "that enemies may speak to each other again, adversaries may join hands, and peoples seek to meet together."[15]

A Voice Crying Out in the World

As it should be clear by now, the art and skill of bridge-building and convening have a strategic intent, primarily to lead people to overcome obstacles in order to focus on consequential matters. In his manner of engagement during the global public health crisis, Pope Francis's strategic intent has focused on promoting the values and principles of Catholic social tradition, notably solidarity, dialogue, the constructive search for peace, and the common good. At key moments during the pandemic, the pope has exercised a prophetic role by reminding the world and its leaders of their common humanity and about how the threat of the coronavirus underscores the existential connection among people across geographical, economic, political, and social boundaries. Accordingly, our common humanity and belonging to one global family serves as an asset in the quest for inclusive, sustainable, and integral development. Furthermore, the pandemic presented the world with a common predicament and underlined the crucial importance of acting as an interdependent community, rather than independent individuals. In other words, multilateralism

---

[15] Francis would have recited this prayer many times as a priest and Bishop of Rome.

takes precedence over unilateralism and any atavistic competition for power. With an authoritative voice that only a handful of world leaders could wield, in his Easter *Urbi et Orbi* message, and at various times during the pandemic, Pope Francis challenged political leaders to ban the words *indifference, self-centeredness, division,* and *forgetfulness* forever. Similarly, he has advocated for international cooperation in the search for a vaccine and treatment and to guarantee that they are considered a global public good that are equitably and universally available to every person in need in every part of the world.

Other areas of importance and urgency have featured regularly in Pope Francis's messages and allocutions, but the coronavirus pandemic gave new and decisive urgency to these issues. For example, Francis has called for a halt to the production and trade of arms. He has appealed for an immediate global cease-fire and moratorium on internecine armed or social conflicts across the world, with special mention of Syria, Yemen, Mozambique, Lebanon, Venezuela, Libya, and Ukraine: "Let us silence the cries of death! No more wars!"[16] According to Francis, from an ethical viewpoint, the production and trade in arms and armed conflict compete with and weaken the government's primary responsibility to make adequate provision for the health and welfare of its citizens. To pay lip service to this responsibility while actively engaged in the business of war amounts to what the pope calls the "functional hypocrisy" of politicians in his interview with Ivereigh.[17] The greatest casualty of such a grave misplacement of priority is human life in all its forms. According to Francis, the tragedy of COVID-19 is a potent reminder that economic and political structures exist to serve life. Thus, the priorities and criteria for reflection, judgment, and action come down to a simple strategy: people and communities *first.* As he wrote to Gallardo, to

---

[16] Pope Francis, Holy Saturday Homily, April 11, 2020 (www.vatican.va).

[17] Pope Francis's interview with Austen Ivereigh, "Take Care of Yourselves for a Future That Will Come," *The Tablet* (April 11, 2020).

upend this priority in favor of economic benefits and political interests at a time of global distress carries the risk of triggering "something like a viral genocide."[18] In the economic realm, the pope's central call relates to the easing of sanctions, debt reduction, or debt forgiveness for poor and indebted nations who are struggling to provide for their citizens at a time when the pandemic has severely strained their limited resources.[19] On the social front, the pope has appealed relentlessly for the protection and promotion of the right of everyone to a dignified access to the means and resources that ensure human flourishing in society. As we saw in the previous chapters, among the categories of the poor and vulnerable people, the preferential focus of Francis is on refugees and migrants, not least because the coronavirus pandemic provided a convenient cover for the surreptitious closure of national borders to migratory people. It would not be necessary to delve into the theme of environmental justice that has received adequate treatment elsewhere as a staple of Pope Francis's gospel of integral ecology, calling attention to the cry of the earth and of the poor.[20]

The foregoing reveals the fulcrum of Francis's message, namely, the importance of maintaining a clear vision of priorities in the unprecedented circumstances of a global crisis. The litany of expressions and soundbites from the pope's pronouncements is memorable: "hold fast to what really counts" (March 19 rosary); "persons, communities and peoples must be put at the center" (Letter to members of social movements); "take seriously the things that are serious" (Palm Sunday homily); "choose what matters in life" (moment of prayer); "'every man for himself' is not a solution" (to Jordi Evole).

---

[18] Gerald O'Connell, "Pope Francis Warns of 'A Viral Genocide' If Governments Put the Economy before People Amid Coronavirus Pandemic," *America*, March 29, 2020 (www.americamagazine.org).

[19] Francis's clarion call echoed the idea of Cardinal Luis Antonio Tagle, the Vatican's Prefect of the Congregation for the Evangelization of Peoples, for a new pandemic "jubilee."

[20] See especially Pope Francis's encyclical *Laudato Si'*.

The coronavirus crisis has demonstrated painful and disturbing pathologies of leadership and laid bare the deficiencies of power. Leaders who fell short have been roundly criticized. Rather than join the chorus of denunciation, Pope Francis has chosen the path of constructive and positive engagement with people who have a political vocation, because he believes that even "the most corrupt leaders . . . are children of God."[21] His preferred approach is not to criticize and expose their weaknesses needlessly, which would only aggravate the plight of the poor and vulnerable. Rather, he has deployed the art and skill of bridge-building strategically and prophetically. Yet, in portraying Francis as a bridge-builder, it is important to correct one likely misconception. For him, bridge-building is hardly a newfound vocation. His entire pontificate has been fundamentally about building and fostering connections across ideological, doctrinal, socioeconomic, and political divides. For making this option he has been showered with adulation and severely criticized in almost equal measure. The pivotal ideas of his pontificate, like the church that goes forth to existential peripheries, church as field hospital, a listening church, and ecclesial synodality, are essential for holding opposing factions and opinions in a healthy and dynamic tension. In this regard, consider his in-flight press conference on a trip from Morocco on March 31, 2019. The trip was consequential not least for the link it helped forge between religions for the sake of world peace, dialogue, freedom, and fraternity. Francis commented that

> We have seen that in the dialogue with you here in Morocco, bridges are needed and it pains us to see people who prefer to build walls. Why are we pained? Because those who build walls will end up as prisoners of the walls they have built. Whereas those who build bridges will go forward. For me, building bridges is

---

[21] General Audience, June 17, 2020 (www.vatican.va).

something almost superhuman, because it requires so much effort.[22]

In the pope's understanding, building walls to separate people does not resolve global problems and crises. Francis went on to offer an instructive anecdote:

> I am deeply touched by a phrase in Ivo Andrić's novel *The Bridge over the Drina*. He says that the bridge is made by God with the wings of angels so that men and women can communicate—between the mountains or the shores of a river—so that men and women can communicate among themselves. The bridge is for human communication. This is very beautiful and I witnessed it here in Morocco. Walls, on the other hand, are against communication; they are for isolation and one becomes a prisoner of those walls.[23]

Alec Guinness, who played Colonel Nicholson in the movie *The Bridge on the River Kwai*, declared with the temerity of a seasoned officer: "One day the war will be over. And I hope that the people that use this bridge in years to come will remember how it was built and who built it. Not a gang of slaves, but soldiers, British soldiers, Clipton, even in captivity." A bridge serves a purpose. Pope Francis sees that purpose as fostering communication, connection, relationship, and solidarity. In the final analysis, a bridge is something that people walk or travel on to cross a gap and reach a new destination. For Francis, pastors "are called *pontifex*, bridges," because they "are the bridges between the people, to whom they belong, and God, to whom they belong by vocation."[24] Indeed, as a pastoral leader, Francis *pontifex* is himself a bridge.

---

[22] Pope Francis, Press Conference on the Return Flight from Rabat to Rome, March 31, 2019 (www.vatican.va).

[23] Ibid.

[24] General Audience, June 17, 2020 (www.vatican.va).

6

Change and Conversion

And no one puts new wine into old wineskins;
otherwise, the wine will burst the skins, and the
wine is lost, and so are the skins; but one puts
new wine into fresh wineskins.

—*Mark 2:22*

This final chapter builds on the considerations of previous chapters. The aim is to explore the challenge of managing change in a time of crisis and uncertainty and the openness incumbent on any organization or community to facilitate the birthing of a different future out of the rubble. In keeping with the subject of this book, I will make the point that leadership plays a crucial role in managing this change, and I will demonstrate how Pope Francis exemplifies the requisite leadership style for such a challenge.

For any institution, change can be complicated and messy depending on how it is handled and the nature of the organization undergoing the process of change. There have already been several attempts to document leadership failures in the face of the coronavirus crisis.[1] Such failures seem to revolve around

---

[1] See Michaela J. Kerrissey and Amy C. Edmondson, "What Good

the inattentiveness of some leaders to the signs of the times and to indications of the necessary changes. The result is a missed opportunity to correct one's course and to make key adjustments to strategy and response. Leadership failures in a time of crisis occur at many levels—global, country, local, organizational, and institutional. It is an attested fact that adaptability and flexibility in a time of crisis and uncertainty do not occur naturally or easily for centuries-old organizations and institutions like the Catholic Church. Change is doubly complex and complicated for the church, which has roots that are deeply embedded in the immutability of tradition, certainty of dogma, and uniformity of ritual. As an institution given to the fierce preservation of an unalterable tradition or the status quo, in the face of a crisis, its leaders can characteristically seem slow, evasive, impassive, and even defensive. Where or when change or reform appears imperative, the institutional reaction might tend to impede, delay, or thwart the course of change.

This reaction has been amply documented in regard to the pernicious clergy sex abuse crisis and the financial scandals inside the Vatican bureaucracy. Pope Francis is aware of this quagmire. He famously compared the task of reforming the Curia or the Vatican bureaucratic apparatus to cleaning Egypt's monumental Sphinx of Giza with a toothbrush. Moreover, Francis is blunt and uncompromising when he admonishes members of his senior leadership team who oppose or sabotage his reform agenda. Oftentimes, he appends unflattering labels to their attitude, rebuking them "as corrupt and cancerous bureaucrats, given to political intrigues, cliques, and complots; seduced by ambition and vainglory; and plagued

Leadership Looks Like during This Pandemic," *Harvard Business Review*, April 13, 2020 (www.hbr.org); Christine Crudo Blackburn and Leslie Ruyle, "How Leadership in Various Countries Has Affected COVID-19 Response Effectiveness," *The Conversation*, May 27, 2020; and Lawrence Hamilton, "What Sets Good and Bad Leaders Apart in the Coronavirus Era?" *The Conversation*, June 7, 2020 (www.theconversation.com).

by 'spiritual Alzheimer's,' 'leprosy,' and 'emptiness.'"[2] Given all his struggles and troubles, papal biographer Austen Ivereigh depicts Francis as a "wounded shepherd."[3] Italian journalist Marco Politi paints a scarier picture in his *Pope Francis among the Wolves.*[4] The sources of Francis's wounds are not all external. Some derive from the fact of human limitation and vulnerability. For someone as open and honest as Francis, it is easy to detect the influence of his personal foibles on his exercise of leadership. To his credit, he rarely deliberately masks, excuses, or deflects attention from his personal weaknesses. But the point of recognizing Francis's limitations is not to apportion blame or belittle his stature. If to err is human, the road to redemption ought to pass through an honest examination of failures, a candid admission of shortcomings, and a firm resolve to learn lessons for the future. Religion calls this process conversion. Alternatively, it is a process of adapting to change with flexibility and creativity. Crises on the scale of the coronavirus pandemic can compel leaders to engage in the process of change and conversion—and Francis demonstrates this reality plainly, with grace and humility.

Church in a Difficult Situation

It is undeniable that the community called church does not adapt easily to change. In the midst of the coronavirus crisis, there has been an instance or two when Pope Francis displayed exasperation with the changes forced upon the institution of the church. One public health measure commonly applied to

[2] Agbonkhianmeghe E. Orobator, SJ, "Francis's Leadership," in *Pope Francis: A Voice for Mercy, Justice, Love, and Care for the Earth*, ed. Barbara E. Wall and Massimo Faggioli (Maryknoll, NY: Orbis Books, 2019), 163–64.

[3] Austen Ivereigh, *Wounded Shepherd: Pope Francis's Struggle to Convert the Catholic Church* (New York: Henry Holt, 2019).

[4] Marco Politi, *Pope Francis among the Wolves: The Inside Story of a Revolution* (New York: Columbia University Press, 2015).

curb the spread of the virus is the ban on public gatherings or the drastic curtailment of the number of people allowed to congregate at any given occasion. In some places that number was as low as two people. Understandably, for an institution like the church, this measure was difficult to comply with. Ordinarily church implies a congregation of people for the purposes of ritual or sacramental worship. The consequence of the restrictions was evident and inevitable: churches would have to close and suspend all worship services. This dilemma was handled differently in different parts of the world. As we saw in the preceding chapter, in some countries, religious leaders disagreed with politicians and public health personnel. The argument of religious leaders in favor of reopening places of worship clashed with the advice of public health experts and government officials. The ensuing tension raised questions around church–state relationships, the scope of political authority, and the meaning of freedom of worship in the time of a global public health crisis. Oftentimes, tension hardened into attitudes of defiance, protestations, and litigiousness. On another level, the controversy revived an age-old debate about how to strike the correct balance between faith and the perception of the benefit of public worship against the risk of infection in collective settings.

For example, in several parts of Africa, in the initial stages of the containment measures, the penchant for congregational worship in the quest for divine intervention was frequently at odds with public health concerns and recommendations. From the previous analysis in this book, it was clear that not many religious leaders understood or accepted the fact that, given the circumstances of the day, congregational worship posed a risk as a potential path for spreading and perpetuating the contagion. Compounding the problem, government advice tended to lack clarity and precision. Initially, while government directives recommended and, in some cases, imposed restrictions on travel, movements, and commercial and recreational activities, such injunctions tended to allow places of worship the prerogative to self-regulate. Only gradually did African countries, starting with Ghana, Uganda, and Rwanda, prescribe and impose stringent measures, including the suspension of all public religious activities without exception.

Even that mandate did not seem to be understood in all cases. Authorities in Uganda arrested two Catholic priests for allegedly violating government orders against any form of public worship. In Kenya, where, as elsewhere, people crave religious assemblies and seek God's help in times of crisis, clarity on regulations about congregating responsibly did not become available until much later in the crisis. Under these circumstances, a sampling of the directives issued by religious leaders creates a feeling of unease at their lack of clarity, consistency, and coordination. Granted, most religious leaders exhorted their followers and ministers to observe strict observance of personal hygiene and adherence to the best evidence-based public health advice. But that was as far as it went. For example, some bishops forbade holding Masses; some imposed restrictions on the number of attendees; and still others simply limited the duration of the worship service. In some instances, it was left to the discretion of the parish priest to decide when, how, and if the sacraments were to be administered, especially to the sick and elderly. One bishop in Nigeria adamantly insisted that "Holy Communion will continue to be given only on the tongue; the hand-shake of peace will continue to be given to those immediately near you." The bishops of Zimbabwe opted to excuse the elderly, children, the sick, and the vulnerable from the obligation to attend Sunday Masses—absolving them of any lingering guilt for failing to attend Mass. Their counterparts in Kenya declared their churches open for business, saying "Our Churches . . . will be the focal point of prayer, where you will find solace and strength from God." In West Africa, Ghana's Catholic Bishops'

Conference was uncompromising, temporarily suspending the public celebration of the Holy Eucharist.

As Easter approached, leaders of religious communities continued to sing a tune of disjointed chords with regard to guidelines and protocols for worship during the ongoing public health crisis. Understandably, they found themselves in uncharted territory with no historical precedent to guide them on how to approach the situation. Uncertainty remained the rule, although some church leaders, like the Archdiocese of Johannesburg in South Africa, announced early on that there was to be no public celebration of Easter services. In this context of generalized confusion and unpredictability, nothing compared to the momentous decision by one of Africa's largest indigenous churches, the Zion Christian Church, to cancel its annual Easter mass pilgrimage to its headquarters in the Moria mountains in the Transvaal in South Africa. The event is by far the single largest gathering of Christians anywhere on the continent, attracting millions of pilgrims from across the Southern Africa region. We can multiply examples, but the point is clear: there was a generalized lack of clear or consistent pastoral guidance on how churchgoers should conduct or fulfill their religious obligations. Clarity did come, but only much later. Without a doubt, like some political leaders, religious leaders moved too slowly in response to the challenges of the times. It is a fair assessment to conclude that they were perennially behind the curve of change and adaptability. On this matter Pope Francis's instinct was perhaps no different from that of his brother bishops and religious leaders, as the following example will demonstrate.

On March 12, 2020, the cardinal-vicar of the Diocese of Rome, Cardinal Angelo De Donatis, decreed that all the churches in the Diocese of Rome should close as part of measures to stop the spread of the coronavirus. This unprecedented decision seemed to rile even the normally unflappable Pope Francis, who has maintained a calm, collected, and confident demeanor amid the coronavirus crisis. The following day, while presiding at the Eucharist in Casa Santa Marta, Francis—the Bishop of Rome—hardly concealed his displeasure at this extraordinary decision to close all churches in *his* diocese. During his reflection, the pope gave the impression that he was unconvinced of the necessity of the closure order. "Drastic measures are not always good," he opined. This terse assertion was enough for Rome's pastors—some Catholic churches in Rome promptly reopened that same day. The Almoner to His Holiness or the head of the Office of Papal Charities, Cardinal Konrad Krajewski, seemed particularly defiant. He kept his titular church, Santa Maria Immacolata, in Rome's Esquiline neighborhood, open and continued to serve cooked meals to the poor and homeless. This episode may seem to contradict the point made in the previous chapter about Pope Francis's positive engagement and cooperation with the efforts of civil and political authorities to tackle the coronavirus pandemic. While there is sufficient ground for upholding this claim, the suggestion that there was a full and uncompromising cooperation does need to be slightly nuanced.

First, it is important to allow for the possibility that the position of cooperation and compliance was not one that Francis adopted without reflection and some struggle. That, perhaps, should not be surprising. Lockdowns and social distancing measures all across the world have not been met with universal and enthusiastic approbation. Quite clearly, the pope was preoccupied with how to discern the proper measures to take to accompany worshippers during the coronavirus crisis without leaving them feeling abandoned, alone, and unaccompanied by their pastors. How to balance the needs of pastoral care with the priorities of public health?

Second, there are other factors to consider. As mentioned in chapter 4, Francis's record of international travel is second only to that of Pope John Paul II. The coronavirus pandemic forced the cancellation of scheduled and planned trips to several countries, including the Asia Pacific countries of Indonesia, Papua New Guinea, and Timor Leste, and to the European countries of Malta, Greece, and Cyprus. Besides these international trips, the Vatican canceled or postponed global gatherings arranged under the auspices of the pope or personally convened by him. The long list of major international events that have been canceled or postponed includes the Economics of Francesco, which is a meeting in Assisi, Italy, of the pope with young economists, entrepreneurs, and change-makers (March 26–28, 2020); the International Global Education Compact in Rome (postponed from May to November 2020); the Fifty-Second International Eucharistic Congress in Budapest, Hungary (September 2020); the World Meeting of Families in Rome (postponed from June 2021 to June 2022); and World Youth Day in Lisbon, Portugal (postponed from August 2022 to August 2023). These cancellations and postponements of major international events would not have left the pope unaffected. Although he judged strict measures as not always beneficial, Francis would eventually adapt to them.

Third, as an economic entity, Vatican City suffered the same fate as other countries. The resultant loss of revenue, collapse of market investments, and diminished voluntary contributions to sustain the operations of the church were enough to trigger drastic budgetary-relieving measures in the Vatican's administrative operations. The Vatican suffered a loss of income from tourists and pilgrims who flock to its museum and historic sites. Estimates by the Vatican Secretariat for the Economy has projected a revenue loss of between 25 percent and 45 percent in 2020. Also, the annual Peter's Pence Collection for the pope's charity for the poor was moved to a later date due to the pandemic. In other parts of the world, some dioceses were compelled to file for bankruptcy protection, while some churches received government loans normally reserved for small businesses. Clergy took a cut on their stipends and salaries, as their sources of revenue dwindled and evaporated due to the coronavirus pandemic.

In one sense, the devastating economic crisis triggered by the pandemic is pushing Pope Francis to experience a dose of his own widely publicized and radical ecclesiological preferences for change. On the one hand, Francis has advocated for a missionary church in opposition to a self-absorbed, self-centered, and self-enclosed church.[5] On the other, he has repeatedly declared his yearning for the emergence of "a Church which is poor and for the poor" (*EG*, 198). The former realizes his dream of a "missionary option," which entails "a missionary impulse capable of transforming everything, so that the Church's customs, ways of doing things, times and schedules, language and structures can be suitably channelled for the evangelization of today's world rather than for her self-preservation" (*EG*, 27). The latter fulfills his ideal of a dirty, hurting, and bruised church that labors alongside the poor and vulnerable people in the streets and existential peripheries (*EG*, 49). Yet, to his credit, rather than wallow in self-pity, lamenting economic and material opportunities lost to containment measures, Pope Francis has maintained a keen focus on the things that matter the most to him. In keeping with his own ethical principles, he has put people and communities ahead of the church's own economic and financial concerns, notwithstanding the difficult situation in which it has found itself—not unlike the pain and suffering endured by the majority of the global community. His approach recalls aspects of a type of leadership that prioritizes the accompaniment of people with closeness, compassion, and solidarity, particularly for the weakest members of society.

Creative Fidelity

When British journalist Austen Ivereigh asked Pope Francis about how he was coping with the uncertainty of the times, personally, practically, and spiritually, the pope did not hide the fact that confinement was a difficult imposition to adapt

---

[5] See *Evangelii gaudium* (*EG*), 28.

to. Rather than capitulate to despair and despondency, Francis spoke of responding with an approach that draws on creativity and innovation. He declared, "I'm living this as a time of great uncertainty. It's a time for inventing, for creativity."[6] As he saw it, a time of crisis offers an opportunity for conversion, personally, but also for the church, for the world, and for the whole of creation. It is a measure of the pope's authenticity and transparency that he does not pretend to live above the frustration of coping with lockdown, confinement, and isolation. Yet, despite indications of being personally irritated and exasperated with impositions and inconveniences caused by the global public health crisis, Pope Francis seemed to graciously embrace the opportunities offered by information communication technology to connect with millions of his followers across the world.

But technology cannot solve everything, of course. To put this situation in perspective, people who know the Vatican and Rome are aware that occasions like Easter are the highest points of pilgrimage and tourism. Even in ordinary times during the year, the pope's events, like public audiences and recitation of the Angelus, attract tens of thousands to Rome and to the Vatican. Thus, for the pope to celebrate the principal feasts and high holy days of Roman Catholicism with a virtual audience and just a handful of people in St. Peter's Basilica was without historical precedent.[7] St. Peter's Basilica and the Square were effectively closed to the public. To say that these celebrations looked different from those that took place prior to the coronavirus pandemic does not quite capture the momentous and historic import of this situation. On such occasions, many correspondents were wont to preface their dispatches with the words "For the first time in living

---

[6] Austen Ivereigh, "Take Care of Yourselves for a Future That Will Come," *The Tablet* (April 11, 2020).

[7] It is worth noting that Muslims and Jews also made changes to their celebration of Ramadan and Passover, respectively.

memory." Besides the pandemic-induced closure of churches globally, if ever there was an epochal liturgical challenge, this reality was cast in bold relief in the near-solitary liturgical rites presided over by Pope Francis in the massive and cavernous principal church of Catholicism. Even when liturgies were held in St. Peter's Basilica, the pope dispensed with nonessential rituals. On Holy Thursday, the Chrism Mass was postponed and the washing of feet and procession at the end of the liturgy were omitted. Good Friday's *Via Crucis* took place on the steps of St. Peter's Basilica rather than in Rome's historic Colosseum. The adoration of the cross by kissing or touching was limited exclusively to the celebrant. There was no procession on Palm Sunday. Francis presided over his Wednesday audience and Sunday recitation of the Angelus and Regina Caeli in the Library of the Apostolic Palace instead of the usual location—the 80,000-capacity St. Peter's Square or the 6,000-seat Paul VI Audience Hall, depending on the weather. From the papal library and his chapel in Casa Santa Marta, these events were livestreamed on TV and virtually on social media to over a million followers.

Needless to say, the official explanation for these adjustments to locations and schedules reflected the extraordinary situation and times of a global public health emergency. The pope understood that such moments called for an extraordinary response. Rather than pick a pointless quarrel with politicians and public health experts over whether or not religion qualifies as an essential service in the middle of a pandemic, he opted to focus on what he saw as the most consequential matters. The pandemic, perhaps, created a propitious occasion for him to experiment with his wish for a radical transformation of everything, so that "times and schedules, language and structures can be suitably channelled for the evangelization of today's world rather than for her [church] self-preservation" (*EG*, 27).

It bears repeating, however, that adaptability to change was not a settled state. Pope Francis would revisit the question of impositions and restrictions and their implications for the life of the church and, in so doing, revealed his ongoing frustration and struggle. In one of his weekly Masses on April 17, 2020, he cautioned against settling too comfortably for a virtual faith in the time of the coronavirus pandemic. For Francis, such situations inherently deprived the Christian community of its cherished assets of personal relationship, physical encounter, and a communal familiarity nourished by the sacraments. Physical presence at the Eucharistic ritual seemed a nonsubstitutable experience; it could not simply be replaced by a virtual presence. According to the pope, spiritual connection does not substitute for physical connection. Having only the former results in a "gnostic" familiarity that satisfies individual preferences but only at the expense of the intimacy of communal familiarity with the Risen Christ. In Francis's imagination and understanding, the fullness of church manifests in the physical congregation around the sacraments, quintessentially in the presence of Christ in the consecrated bread and wine of the Eucharist. While a virtual congregation or worship may approximate this ecclesial reality, it is not church in the real sense of the term, that is, a ritualized group activity that allows people to experience, express, and celebrate their faith in person. Rather, for Francis, "this is the church in a difficult situation."[8] Whether or not the pope realized it at the time, his reasoning echoed almost verbatim a somewhat dated statement by the defunct Pontifical Council for Social Communications:

> Virtual reality is no substitute for the Real Presence of Christ in the Eucharist, the sacramental reality of the other sacraments, and shared worship in a flesh-and-blood human community. There are no sacraments on the Internet; and even the religious experiences possible

---

[8] Carol Glatz, "Pope Says Living Faith without Sacraments, Community Is Dangerous," *National Catholic Reporter*, April 17, 2020 (www.ncronline.org).

there by the grace of God are insufficient apart from real-world interaction with other persons of faith.[9]

For its author(s), however, this statement did not discount the multiple advantages and benefits of the Internet for church mission and ministry, particularly among young people. At best, the Internet is a complementary tool for experiencing the sacraments and for predisposing, preparing, and leading people to a concrete experience of community.

Not a few theologians have expressed similar sentiments and opinions in the context of the coronavirus pandemic. Editor in Chief Robert Mickens of the international Catholic online magazine *La Croix* articulated his displeasure and disapproval of alternative virtual ways of continuing to "do" sacraments. "Let's be clear," he stated categorically, "we cannot really 'participate' in a virtual Mass any more than we can share a virtual handshake, hug or kiss. Some things demand real presence. It's amazing how many Catholic priests and people seem to have forgotten this."[10] To be fair, aside from the drawbacks of online worship, Mickens's larger point consisted of a critique of an insipid "clerical activism" redolent of an insatiable and relentless obsession to "keep doing" sacraments over the Internet and on TV. Such an activist approach to sacramentality misses the opportunity to allow people to "stop" and to simply experience the consolation of just "being" in the moment, even if that moment was imposed by confinement measures against the spread of COVID-19. However, Mickens seems to overlook the fact that as many as two-thirds of the world's population experienced the "stop" as an involuntary situation of confinement, isolation, and

---

[9] Pontifical Council for Social Communications, "The Church and Internet," February 2, 2002, 9 (www.vatican.va).

[10] Robert Mickens, "A Church (and World) in Denial That Just Can't Stop Itself," *La Croix International*, April 24, 2020 (www.international.la-croix.com).

restriction, with serious personal, psychological, and economic costs. Under such circumstances, perhaps it would be naïve to think that most people would happily have embraced the coronavirus crisis as an opportunity to slow down, reflect, and simply just be—a luxury that only the economically secure and socially privileged could afford. For the poor and vulnerable, lockdown posed an existential threat: a matter of life and death. Finally, Mickens does not seem to have taken into account the importance of not judging or determining the value of virtual worship solely as a matter of abstract theological disputation.

Against the backdrop of a catastrophic crisis laden with pain, suffering, and anxiety, the frenetic pastoral reflections and frenzied theological debates on the topic of the "virtual" celebration of the Eucharist and the related issues of the degree of "realness" or "presence" required for validity and the proliferation of Eucharistic tourism seem merely to be the indulgent petty squabbles of armchair theologians. To his credit, Pope Francis did not stray into such zones of conceptual and theological sterility. Despite voicing his frustration, Francis made a deliberate choice to continue to exercise his ministry of compassion, consolation, and spiritual accompaniment even when the means of being close to people were imperfect, limited, and virtual. While it would be unfair to reduce Francis's noteworthy decision to continue pastoral ministry in the time of a pandemic to just an act of clerical activism, a pertinent question to ask would be whether the relocation of liturgical practices to informal and domestic settings, be they virtual or physical, is embraced as an opportunity for real creativity and meaningful change—one that values, prioritizes, and creates space for the sacramental and liturgical leadership of laypeople, particularly women—or merely as a temporary virtualization of routine patterns of worship orchestrated by an elite corps of clerics. To address this question would result in a digression from the aim and scope of this book.

To extend the argument a little further, though, there are many ways of interpreting and understanding the pope's ecclesiological perspective as manifested by his remarks about the limitation of a virtual faith. It is important to undertake such interpretation within the context of his situation in time. That Francis felt personally the frustration and exasperation of the involuntary confinement dictated by the needs of public health is evident in his remarks about the inadequacy of a virtual worship. Some, though, would interpret his remarks as further proof of a recalcitrant hierarchy and its incurable craving for an ecclesial arrangement that subjects the sacramental life of the church inexorably to the control of ordained ministers and so excludes the possibility of lay participation and involvement in ministerial leadership. While this argument makes sense theologically, it bears too much weight to rest solely on one instance of the pope's expression of personal disaffection. Actually, Pope Francis spoke of "the ideal of the church" that is always with the people and celebrating sacraments. He did not oppose that ideal to "a church in a difficult situation" due to extraordinary circumstances of the time. Again, despite the challenges, Francis adapted to the times and continued to minister as priest and bishop and leader of a global faith community.

The pope who had complained about shuttering churches and the curtailment of in-person sacramental ministry nevertheless held his discontent in check out of care and respect for the health and well-being of others and in compliance with containment measures introduced by civil authorities to limit the spread of the coronavirus. Instead, he creatively embraced digital technology as a means of fulfilling his leadership and sacramental duties to his global audience of followers. By his own self-assessment and admission to Ivereigh, the daily livestreaming of the Eucharist that he presided over in Casa Santa Marta chapel, the moment of prayer on March 27, and the work of the Office of Papal Charities demonstrate inventive ways of accompanying and maintaining closeness with the people of God. As he explained it, "I'm living this as a time of great uncertainty. It's a time for inventing, for creativity."[11]

Creativity entails the constructive and responsible use of freedom. And creativity does not need to be at odds with tradition and orthodoxy. Pope Francis alluded to this notion of freedom in the time of crisis in his interview with Ivereigh, by telling an anecdote of a somewhat flustered bishop worried about how to give absolution without direct contact with patients sickened by COVID-19. By way of counsel, Francis offered four simple words: "Fulfill your priestly duty."[12] The pope's response was genuine enough to liberate the bishop's conscience and give free rein to his ministerial creativity. Another related example is worth mentioning. In Italy, which was one of the epicenters of the coronavirus pandemic, a local bishop gave permission to a group of six doctors to distribute communion to patients infected by the coronavirus in order to provide both spiritual and physical care at Easter. Nothing in this practice contravenes church stipulation. The latter allows for the institution of Extraordinary Ministers of the Eucharist to meet specific needs. Positively construed, the bishop's decision is both an example of innovative thinking in a time of crisis and an expression of creative fidelity to church practice and tradition. And the response was one of grateful enthusiasm. As one of the doctor-ministers said, "It was one of the most beautiful experiences I have lived in my life as a man, as a Christian and as a doctor."[13] The patient-communicants would likely have concurred. This approach of creative fidelity validates one of the theses of this book, that from a leadership perspective extraordinary times warrant extraordinary measures. Such measures entail concrete changes. As the foregoing

---

[11] Ivereigh, "Take Care of Yourselves for a Future That Will Come."

[12] Ibid.

[13] Junno Arocho Esteves, "Bishop Allows Doctors to Give Communion to Coronavirus Patients," NCR Online, April 15, 2020.

analysis shows, this is a principle that Pope Francis has understood and applied to good effect. In the account of another
doctor-minister, the idea was inspired by Francis's call for doctors and medical professionals "to play the role of intermedi-
aries of the church for people who are suffering." There is no
hint here whatsoever of clerical activism.

During the coronavirus crisis, Pope Francis introduced and
authorized other changes, including the easing of the process
of granting absolution for people stricken by COVID-19 and
those who cared for them. Additionally, the pope approved
two new liturgical texts for use during the pandemic, namely,
a special "Mass in the Time of Pandemic" and an insert in
the list of petitions in the Good Friday liturgy invoking God's
compassion for those suffering the consequences of the pandemic. Perhaps nothing was more visually surreal and stun-
ning than the image of the pope standing in the study window
of the papal apartment with a sprawling vista of an empty St.
Peter's Square, imparting his weekly blessing virtually on a
worldwide audience. The upshot is that with the right kind of
leadership, change can happen for an institution as venerable
as the Catholic Church, which, as Francis has argued, is not "a
museum of memories" (*Gaudete et exsultate* (*GE*), 139; *GE*,
58; *EG*, 95). And when this change happens, it can enhance
rather than undermine the resilience, adaptability, and flexibility of the institution concerned.

Co-architect of the Future

Adaptability and flexibility in a time of crisis and the atten-
dant changes inspire creative fidelity, even when an institution is in a difficult situation. Also, these qualities represent a
strategic openness to the future. Only when an institution has
successfully navigated this process of change, even if reluc-
tantly and hesitatingly, can it contribute validly and credibly
to the birthing of a new and future reality. As Pope Francis
told Ivereigh, a crisis imposes an imperative of profound and

meticulous preparation in view of assuming the monumental task of tending "a future that will come." The facilitation of the discernment and imagination of what that future would look like is a constitutive function of leadership. Thus, for Francis, no matter how concrete and visceral the grim reality of pain, suffering, and death is for victims of the global public health crisis, it cannot lock down definitively and permanently their hope for a new life. As was the case for the women of Jerusalem on their early morning pilgrimage to the tomb of the crucified Christ, the stone that sealed the tomb would eventually be rolled away and life would reemerge from the darkness of death with shining splendor. Curiously but not unsurprisingly, for the pope, the bearers and architects of this hope are not necessarily the people in positions of power, privilege, and prerogative. The creators of a future full of hope will be doctors, nurses, people stocking the supermarket shelves, cleaners, caretakers, people who transport goods, public security officials, volunteers, women religious, grandparents, teachers, and so many others who are routinely undervalued but are essential to the functioning of society.

As government and civil authorities contemplated various options and permutations for easing restrictions on business, commercial, and recreational activities necessitated by the coronavirus pandemic, Pope Francis presented a meditative essay, "*Un plan para resucitar*" ("A plan to resurrect"), on the online Spanish-language religious weekly *Vida Nueva* (April 17, 2020). Francis's vision for a post-COVID-19 world, which will be discussed at more length in the Conclusion of this book, does not peddle pious exhortations or useless nostrums. Nor is it limited to responding to the immediacy and urgency of the moment of crisis. Responding to concrete needs and preparing for the future are mutually reinforcing options. The task of shaping rather than simply responding to the future entails a monumental commitment to planning and executing concrete initiatives in the aftermath of the pandemic. Although governments and international governmental and nongovernmental organizations bear the greatest responsibility, Francis does not exempt the church from this duty. Accordingly, the pope entrusted the task of planning and contributing to the future to his department for the Service of Integral Human Development, led by Cardinal Peter Turkson. The wide-ranging purview of the department encompasses coordinating the initiatives of the global network of churches, humanitarian organizations, and Vatican diplomatic representations; facilitating collaboration across the various departments, agencies, and academic platforms of the Vatican to create synergy and efficiency; promoting effective communication and awareness-building; initiating constructive partnerships with governments and international multilateral agencies; and soliciting and generating the necessary financial and material resources to accomplish the department's task. In essence, just as Pope Francis has been deeply involved in responding to the challenges of the coronavirus pandemic, so is he invested in the task of designing, building, and birthing "a future that will come" after the global health emergency.

The liturgical lockdown occasioned by the coronavirus pandemic has unsettled and disempowered many believers and disoriented and paralyzed many pastors. Some theologians and commentators continue to debate the validity and merit of adapting liturgical and sacramental celebration to digital platforms and formats like the Internet, social media, and cable TV. Although Pope Francis underwent his own conversion to virtual forms of ministry, it was neither automatic nor absolute. On the whole, judging by Francis's performance, it is a fair assessment to conclude that online or virtual worship did not seem as deviant an option as some would make it out to be, especially in the extraordinary circumstances of a contagious and lethal pandemic. After all, at the beginning of the crisis, the pope had indicated the methodology of his ministry by declaring, "I will accompany you from here." The successful fulfillment of this commitment could only be made possible through a creative adaptation and use of digital technology and virtual means. That is not to insinuate that it settles the deeper ethical question of the affordability and accessibility of the Internet. Remote work, telehealth, and teleworship further amplify underlying socioeconomic inequalities and a vast digital divide heavily weighted against the poor and the underprivileged.

A crisis of pandemic proportion can force leaders to make changes of historic proportion. Pope Francis prefers the more theologically suited language of conversion. As evidenced by Francis's leadership during the coronavirus pandemic, adaptability, flexibility, and creativity are prerequisites of change. Granted, this process of change does not come naturally and easily for centuries-old institutions like the church. For any leader, part of the process of leading and managing change entails, to use the pope's own words on March 27, 2020, discerning, differentiating, and choosing between essentials and non-essentials, "what matters and what passes away . . . what is necessary from what is not."[14] Without discounting the risks and threats of the global public health crisis, Francis has demonstrated the possibility of discerning opportunities and drawing lessons from the crisis. When creatively and courageously engaged, crises offer a privileged moment of conversion (or *metanoia*) for the church, the world, and the whole of creation.

---

[14] "Extraordinary Moment of Prayer Presided Over by Pope Francis," March 27, 2020 (www.vatican.va).

Conclusion

A New Vision of What Is Possible

See, I am making all things new.

—*Revelation 21:5*

At the end of the fourth gospel, the Johannine author(s) declares that "There are also many other things that Jesus did; if every one of them were written down, I suppose that the world itself could not contain the books that would be written" (Jn 21:25). Another conclusion to the gospel, appearing in the preceding chapter, adopts a slightly nuanced perspective: "Now Jesus did many other signs in the presence of his disciples, which are not written in this book. But these are written so that you may come to believe that Jesus is the Messiah, the Son of God, and that through believing you may have life in his name" (Jn 20:30–31). From the former ending, which concedes the impossibility of compiling a complete narrative of the deeds of Jesus Christ, and the latter, which highlights the missionary and exhortatory intent of the narrative, one can appreciate analogously the features and intent of this short book on lessons in leadership in a time of crisis.

Several characteristics and limitations of this account should be acknowledged. Far from being a comprehensive narrative, it takes a snapshot of Pope Francis's comportment as a leader at a particular time during the coronavirus pandemic. This book is neither an unofficial biography nor a historical chronicle of the life and deeds of the pope. My intent is partly motivational and partly pedagogical. I have written this book in order to distill important lessons on leadership in a time of crisis based on a careful observation of Francis—his words and actions, preferences and priorities. I do not concern myself with elaborating or debating theories. Rather, I observe the pope's activities, sift through his pronouncements, and scrutinize his attitudes in the rapidly unfolding circumstances of a global health emergency. This modest work is an experiment in education in moral and imaginative leadership. In my opinion, it has generated several important insights that can be applied to the most ordinary circumstances of human life and endeavor. It has also engendered numerous questions that warrant further debate and consideration beyond that which I have undertaken.

The severe acute respiratory syndrome coronavirus 2 (SARS-CoV-2), the virus that causes coronavirus disease 2019 (COVID-19), is not the first plague to traumatize the world. And in all likelihood, it will not be the last. This global public health crisis has a lot in common with

> other such outbreaks throughout human history: the staggering costs in terms of lives and livelihoods; the anguish—physical, mental, emotional, and spiritual— afflicting millions, even billions, of people; and the stress and strains put on all, but especially on those whose calling it is to serve, protect, treat, and/or care for others.[1]

At its core, though, the crisis presents a serious test of leadership. There is abundant evidence to substantiate the powerful

---

[1] Stephen Bullivant, *Catholicism in the Time of Coronavirus* (Park Ridge, IL: Word on Fire, 2020), 3 (www.wordonfire.org).

assertion of the director general of the World Health Organization, Tedros Adhanom Ghebreyesus, that "The greatest threat we face now is not the virus itself, it's the lack of global solidarity, and global leadership."[2] This threat persists because the coronavirus is still with us even as country after country has elected to ease restrictions and embarked on a real-time experiment in learning how to live sensibly with the virus. There is no guarantee against a further resurgence of cases globally, with consequences just as devastating or even worse than the initial occurrence. The recommended attitude remains one of prudence, caution, and social distancing. Thus, at this stage, any conclusion must be tentative. Without a doubt, the combination of the high transmissibility of COVID-19 and its lethal toll has unleashed a global tsunami of dire social, economic, and political consequences, perhaps more so than any previously known pandemic. The full human, social, economic, political, and ecological cost of this global public health crisis may not be known for a long time.

In time, the coronavirus catastrophe may eventually seem like a watershed in global history: BC-19 (before COVID-19) and AC-19 (after COVID-19). Although many people harbor the hope of returning to a prepandemic normality, a better-informed consensus concedes that there will be no normal way of life to which humanity will return after the coronavirus pandemic has been defeated or at least held in check. There has been a slow-dawning realization of the variety of changes provoked by the coronavirus pandemic for people, communities, and countries across the world to such an extent that life no longer seems normal. Humanity is adjusting to a new reality wounded and chastened by an invisible enemy. Every pestilence tells a story and leaves its scars. The story profiles heroes and heroines who fought gallantly to overcome its menace. The scars run deep, with heartrending memories of pain,

---

[2] Tedros Adhanom Ghebreyesus, "Address to World Government Summit," June 22, 2020 (www.who.int).

loss, and broken lives and livelihoods. As Pope Francis told an audience of health care personnel from the Italian Lombardy region, "The pandemic left a deep mark in the life of people and the history of communities."[3] Humanity has historically emerged from each cycle of plague fewer in number, but more resilient and determined to press on, even when the lessons were sometimes neither discerned with clarity nor learned with alacrity. As humanity cautiously navigates a postpandemic era, it is important to preserve the memory of the collective experience of COVID-19 and to avoid a panic-and-forget approach. In other words, it is important to learn the lessons of this crisis. "This way, we will emerge from this crisis spiritually and morally stronger," Francis told the Italian medics.

This book rests on the premise that the story of the coronavirus pandemic positively highlights the leadership of Pope Francis. The manner in which the pope leads remains open to scrutiny and to the possibility of drawing differing conclusions, but I have taken the view that Francis provides a reliable global reference point for drawing the lessons of the coronavirus pandemic from the vantage point of leadership. In sum, the manner in which he has handled the crisis has also exemplified a discernible style of effective leadership and thus offers instructive lessons for leadership in a time of crisis. Although I made a deliberate choice to study Pope Francis in the context of a world in distress, he is not alone in dealing with the extreme challenges of that world. Just as easily and interestingly, a similar study could—and I hope will—be made of other leaders with comparable results. There are quasi-objective and objective criteria for identifying those who have acquitted themselves creditably and honorably well and the effectiveness of government responses to the coronavirus crisis.[4]

---

[3] "Pope Thanks Italian Doctors and Health Care Workers for Heroic Service during Pandemic," *Vatican News*, June 20, 2020 (www.vaticannews.va).

[4] "Covid-19 Has Given Most World Leaders a Temporary Rise

In all likelihood, future studies would include Governor Andrew Cuomo of New York, Prime Minister Jacinda Ardern of New Zealand, and centenarian Captain Tom Moore, who raised millions of dollars for UK's National Health Service during the coronavirus pandemic by walking laps in his small garden to mark his one hundredth birthday. A longer list would include President Tsai Ing-wen of Taiwan; German Chancellor Angela Merkel; Denmark's prime minister, Mette Frederiksen; and Sanna Marin, the Finnish prime minister. This list reveals an unmistakable and significant gender quotient. Although current studies recognize the crucial importance of decisive leadership in managing the coronavirus crisis, gender has emerged as an incontrovertible determinant of success. This factor warrants further study to distill the appropriate lessons.[5]

Case studies in leadership during the pandemic would also mention other (presently unnamed) leaders who put politics, cronyism, authoritarianism, and self-interest ahead of the common good and people's welfare. What is evident, as demonstrated in this book, is that the coronavirus crisis has exposed

---

in Popularity," *The Economist*, May 9, 2020 (www.economist.com); Thomas Hale, Noam Angrist, Beatriz Kira, Anna Petherick, Toby Phillips, and Samuel Webster, "Variation in Government Responses to COVID-19," Version 6.0. Blavatnik School of Government Working Paper, May 25, 2020 (www.bsg.ox.ac.uk/covidtracker).

[5] Jon Henley and Eleanor Ainge Roy, "Are Female Leaders More Successful at Managing the Corona-Virus Crisis?" *The Guardian*, April 25, 2020 (www.theguardian.com); "Covid-19: Where Women Lead, Coronavirus Dies," *Daily Nation,* June 16, 2020 (www.nation.ke); Rebecca Formana, Rifat Atun, Martin McKeec, and Elias Mossialos, "12 Lessons Learned from the Management of the Coronavirus Pandemic," *Health Policy* 124, no. 6 (June 2020): 577–80; Ahmed Mohammed Obaid Al Saidi, Fowsiya Abikar Nur, Ahmed Salim Al-Mandhari, Maha El Rabbat, Assad Hafeez, and Abdinasir Abubakar, "Decisive Leadership Is a Necessity in the COVID-19 Response," *The Lancet*, July 3, 2020 (doi.org/10.1016/S0140-6736(20)31493-8).

the recklessness and excesses of some leaders. While it is true that authoritarian leaders tend to proliferate during crises, because they prey on people's vulnerability and craving for strong leadership, such regimes surreptitiously end up eroding personal freedoms under the guise of providing protection and safety. The coronavirus pandemic gave some regimes an opportunity to use emergency powers as a weapon to suppress dissent and control the population. Sadly, they overlooked the truth that power does not equate to leadership, and when the former is detached from the latter, it exists only to serve and promote a narrow self-interest at the expense of the people. Wielding power may gratify its agent, but exercising leadership serves a higher purpose. The former is common but the latter less so. This study unmasks self-interested power and highlights a kind of leadership in the service of life and human flourishing.

Between the two categories of leaders mentioned in the preceding paragraphs, some have been rewarded with electoral success, while others lost credibility among their people. Not being an elected politician, Pope Francis has been spared such a reckoning. Nevertheless, his approach to the coronavirus crisis contrasts sharply and discernibly with that of incompetent, short-sighted, and capricious leaders, and complements the approach of competent, conscientious, and compassionate leaders. The latter group—to varying degrees—has displayed some of the leadership qualities highlighted in this book. Not being an elected political leader may be to Francis's advantage—he is not encumbered with any compulsion to indulge in empty spectacles, project a false sense of security, or feign concern for people. Yet for all the tribute paid to his leadership style in this book there is no suggestion of perfection in his response to the crisis. In some concrete instances, we have seen the foibles and exasperation of a pope who famously described himself as a sinner, not in a figurative sense, he insisted, but as "the most accurate definition."[6] Nonetheless, it would be fair to conclude that he, too, has acquitted himself honorably well as a pastoral and prophetic leader worthy of emulation. In addition to what I have already explored in this short book, it is important to also take into account the following considerations.

The leadership lessons, qualities, or principles identified and held up for emulation in this book are not an application of a set of sophisticated theories. I have deliberately avoided categorizing these lessons according to the customary taxonomy of "soft" vs. "hard" skills. I find this division unhelpful in this context, since the crisis that forms the subject of this book does not present under the kind of sharp demarcations that require discrete and neatly circumscribed skills. Besides, there is not a hint that Pope Francis follows a blueprint, a self-help instruction, or a do-it-yourself manual—much less that he tries to apply a theoretical or conceptual model of leadership. The lessons pointed out in this book reflect aspects of his theological imagination and deep personal conviction. Hence, while they may appear unstructured and "soft," they are neither capricious nor inconsequential. If anything has come to characterize Francis's style of leadership, it is his inimitable proclivity for an inclusive pastoral accompaniment that reflects the image of God as mercy, compassion, and tenderness.

Long before the outbreak of COVID-19, and even before his election as pope, Francis habitually indulged the gospel command to give preference to the poor, the crippled, the lame, and the blind when composing a guest list for banquets and dinner parties—in other words, people who have neither the capacity nor the means to return the favor (see Lk 14:12–14). On his birthdays, the pope has partied with migrants, homeless people, detainees, and prisoners. During his papal walkabouts he has singled out people with disabilities, people afflicted with debilitating diseases, and children for a special

---

[6] Antonio Spadaro, "A Big Heart Open to God: An Interview with Pope Francis," *America*, September 30, 2013 (www.americamagazine.org).

hug. Far from being a textbook exercise, Francis's approach to leadership is a clear reflection of his character and faith. Authentic leadership comes from a place of depth—and, in a time of crisis, when lives are at stake, it calls for leading from the heart.

In the midst of the coronavirus pandemic, neither Pope Francis nor his aides delivered regular press briefings. Yet Francis has remained visible to a global audience to deliver a message of hope. According to the testimony of British Ambassador to the Holy See Sally Axworthy at an occasion to honor the church's contribution to tackling COVID-19 worldwide, "Pope Francis gave us hope in the dark days when the virus first struck."[7] The pope has kept on ministering to the needs of humanity even if constrained by the statutory confinement measures and limited to available means of information communication technology. It is a fair assumption that Francis was under no compulsion to maintain high public visibility during the coronavirus pandemic. Taking account of his age as a predisposing factor, he could have opted for a strict isolation far from harm's way, while clinging to his own security, like the unhealthy church he abhors and criticizes.[8] It is a measure and mark of compassionate leadership to resist the temptation to retreat to a comfortable and sterile zone in order to wait out a tempestuous plague or crisis. Granted, there were reported cases of the coronavirus outbreak within the Vatican City State and in the pope's Casa Santa Marta guesthouse, and of course adequate precaution would have been taken to protect the octogenarian pope from exposure to the virus. Although the infections in the Vatican have been on a relatively small scale, the due acknowledgment of the presence of cases of coronavirus

---

[7] Deborah Lubov, "For Queen's Birthday, British Ambassador to Holy See Hosts Virtual Afternoon Tea to Honor Church's Contribution to Tackling Covid-19," *Zenit*, June 6, 2020 (www.zenit.org).

[8] See *EG*, 49.

there is also an indication of transparency. And in a time of crisis, transparency is at the service of credible leadership.

While it is true that in other situations, such as clergy sex abuse, transparency and accountability have been lacking, the coronavirus pandemic seems different. The reasons for this disparity vary, but three in particular come to mind. First, as countless revelations show, unlike the pandemic, clergy sexual abuse runs deep in the church's history and hierarchy, aided by a deliberate practice of denial and cover-up that effectively concealed the evil. Second, the need to protect the institution of the church seemed paramount relative to the moral imperative and gospel injunction to do no harm to minors and vulnerable people. Third, perhaps it is easier to focus on an external threat, like the pandemic, than a self-inflicted one that has seriously sullied the credibility of the church and several of its leaders. The main point here is, however, that authentic leadership is visible, engaged, and transparent; and, in a time of crisis, it does not operate or float above the vicissitude of ordinary circumstances of life.

As I have pointed out in this book, Pope Francis's intervention in the coronavirus crisis has assumed many forms. Spiritual exhortation, reflections, messages, and moments of prayer were complemented and reinforced by symbolic gestures, including reaching out to political leaders and civic authorities to offer support and encouragement. Also, Francis's intervention was accompanied by concrete initiatives. In the previous chapter, I discussed the work of the papal department for the Service of Integral Human Development, the body tasked with leading the Vatican's initiatives in response to the global public health crisis. In addition to this response, there are several recorded examples of the pope taking action to alleviate the pain and suffering of people. For the pope, prayer is a form of action, as is charity, and word is complemented by witness. In his mind, the inseparability of both is never in doubt: "Prayer to God and solidarity with the poor and suffering are inseparable. . . . Time devoted to prayer can never become an alibi for neglecting our neighbor in need."[9] In the middle of the crisis, Pope Francis established an Emergency Fund with the aim of supporting people and communities impacted by the spread of COVID-19 in the developing countries of the Global South. Not only did the pope create the fund, he also made the first contribution of $750,000. Francis would later create another fund, *Gesu Divino Lavoratore* (Jesus the Divine Worker), dedicated to easing the pain and suffering caused by the pandemic for the vulnerable, poor, and informal sector workers in the city of Rome, with an initial donation of €1 million. These initiatives mirror on a miniscule scale the staggering sums of money committed by governments and international financial organizations to mitigate the macro- and microeconomic impacts of the pandemic globally.

Ordinarily, the pope's charitable and humanitarian interventions are delivered through the Papal Almoner or the Office of Papal Charities. This office is responsible for offering charitable assistance to the poor in the name of the pope, and traces its origins back to Pope Gregory X (1271–76). Traditionally, the Almoner serves the needs of the homeless, refugees, and poor in Rome with donations of food and supplies received from individuals and organizations. Strikingly, during the pandemic, in the name of Pope Francis, Papal Almoner Cardinal Krajewski formally requested all 250 bishops, cardinals, and high-ranking prelates working and/or resident in the Vatican to donate their entire month's stipend to support the Papal Fund to assist with the coronavirus pandemic. For rationale, Cardinal Krajewski opined that "Vatican officials should somehow participate in the pain that so many families feel these days losing loved ones."[10] His appeal seemed to have paid off as

---

[9] "Message of Pope Francis for 2020 World Day of the Poor" (June 13, 2020), 6.

[10] Paulina Guzik, "'Alms Need to Hurt'—Papal Almoner Explains Call for Vatican Prelates to Donate during Crisis," *Crux*, April 8, 2020 (www.cruxnow.com).

evidenced by the recorded number of items donated by the Almoner, which included 600,000 masks to assist with efforts to combat COVID-19 in the provinces of Hubei, Zhejiang, and Fujian, China; more than 65 ventilators and respirators to hospitals in the areas most affected by the coronavirus pandemic; and 2,500 COVID-19 screening kits to the Ministry of Health in Gaza, Palestine. Overall, this response reinforces the point made in chapter 2 about the preferential option for the poor and vulnerable and Francis's solicitude for them during the pandemic. Also, these actions align with the pope's broader theological vision of the church-as-field-hospital, aspects of which include listening to and accompanying the poor and vulnerable with compassion, mercy, and tenderness. In a time of crisis, rhetoric does not suffice; instead, word combines with personal witness as a manifestation of compassion for and solidarity with the pain and suffering of others.

Although it is important to remember a pandemic as devastating as COVID-19 and honor the memory of its stupefying number of victims, it is normal for individuals, communities, and countries to imagine the shape of a world beyond the plague. Historically, in the aftermath of major global catastrophes, it has been necessary to create international coalitions to spearhead the process of recovery, reconstruction, and restoration. Europeans of a certain generation would be familiar with one such successful and historic initiative, namely, the Marshall Plan or European Recovery Program (April 1948–December 1951), which was a US-led initiative to rebuild Europe following the tragedy of World War II. There is a plethora of post-pandemic recovery plans across the world that are specifically designed to open up and repair the economies shaken, shuttered, or shattered by the pandemic. Many such plans have been conceived by individual countries; a few pull together the collective strength of geopolitical blocs. Expectedly, the emphasis has been on economic regeneration involving unprecedented sums of money commonly designated as stimulus packages. As we saw in chapter 6, Pope Francis has developed an analogous plan—"A plan to resurrect."[11] "Plan" is perhaps a misnomer for the title of a profoundly theological and spiritual reflection on issues of deeper concern in the wake of the coronavirus pandemic—Francis's plan applies his interpretation of the biblical narrative of Jesus's resurrection to the global public health crisis. Nonetheless, it merits serious consideration.

The pope observes that during a crisis, hope and joy are weighed down by pain and uncertainty. In the bleakness of a pandemic, "we experience a *famine of hope*," he declared in his Pentecost homily.[12] Yet a renewed faith, an audacious hope, and a selfless love are constitutive ingredients of any plan to overcome the assault set off by the global crisis. Pope Francis models his uplifting and hopeful reflection on the example of the courageous women of Jerusalem who made an early morning pilgrimage to the tomb of the crucified Lord. Undeterred by fear and obstacles, they did what they felt they could and were obliged to do to tend to the body of the crucified Lord. Unbeknownst to them, the resurrected Lord had preceded them and waited for their arrival to reward their faith, hope, and charity with his intense joy and consoling presence. However, the women did not keep the joy of the resurrection to themselves; they shared it enthusiastically with their fellow disciples, because salvation is eminently communal. In this sense, as Francis declared on the Pentecost Vigil in 2020, "The lesson we have learned" in the coronavirus crisis is that "we are a single humanity. We cannot save ourselves by ourselves. No one saves him or herself alone. No one."[13] In light of this lesson, Francis's plan for rising up again is rooted in the princi-

---

[11] "*Un plan para resucitar*" (A Plan to Resurrect), essay published by Pope Francis on the online Spanish-language religious weekly *Vida Nueva* (April 17, 2020).

[12] Homily of His Holiness Pope Francis, Solemnity of Pentecost, May 31, 2020 (www.vatican.va).

[13] Video Message of His Holiness Pope Francis on the Occasion of the Pentecost Vigil Promoted by Charis (Catholic Charismatic Renewal International Service), May 30, 2020 (www.vatican.va).

ples of compassion, collaboration, cooperation, and solidarity. These values are nonnegotiable for a profound, meaningful, and long-lasting postpandemic renewal of humanity in order to "make all things new" (Rv 21:5).

Furthermore, Pope Francis's plan for rising up again is not designed for the church; primarily, it is a plan for a postpandemic world. However, it draws on the resources of faith and fulfills the church's prophetic mission:

> The Church certainly has no comprehensive solutions to propose, but by the grace of Christ, she can offer her witness and her gestures of charity. She likewise feels compelled to speak out on behalf of those who lack life's basic necessities. For the Christian people, to remind everyone of the great value of the common good is a vital commitment, expressed in the effort to ensure that no one whose human dignity is violated in its basic needs will be forgotten.[14]

In the logic of this plan, the time of crisis doubles as a Kairos moment for a Spirit-inspired creativity and "a new imagination of what is possible."[15] As Francis told Austen Ivereigh, a significant part of his plan consists of an appeal for the active preservation of global consciousness and collective memory: "But let us not lose our memory once all this is past, let us not file it away and go back to where we were."[16] Yet we do not preserve memory simply for the sake of selectively remember-

---

[14] "Message of Pope Francis for 2020 World Day of the Poor," 5.

[15] Pope Francis, "*Un plan para resucitar*" (A Plan to Resurrect). Similar to Pope Francis's vision, in his analysis of the postpandemic world, Slavoj Žižek envisions the possibility of the emergence of "an alternate society, a society beyond nation-state, a society that actualizes itself in the forms of global solidarity and cooperation." *Pandemic! COVID-19 Shakes the World* (New York: Polity Press, 2020), 39.

[16] Austen Ivereigh, "Take Care of Yourselves for a Future That Will Come," *The Tablet* (April 11, 2020).

ing and commemorating events consigned to the past. Construed as an ethical imperative, memory serves the future; remembrance aids the imagination of new possibilities. Also, memory begets hope for a better future. This idea is at the heart of Pope Francis's message to the Catholic Charismatic Renewal International Service on the vigil of Pentecost 2020:

> When we get out of this pandemic, we will not be able to continue doing what we have been doing, and how we have been doing it. No, everything will be different. All the suffering will have been useless if we do not build together a fairer, more equitable, more Christian society, not in name, but in reality, a reality that leads us to Christian conduct. If we do not work to end the pandemic of poverty in the world, with the pandemic of poverty in the country of each one of us, in the city where each one of us lives, this time will have been in vain.[17]

In chapter 2, I argued against the false narrative of the coronavirus pandemic as the great social leveler or equalizer. Nevertheless, it is a noteworthy dimension of the pandemic that COVID-19 breached the barricades of the highest corridors of power and infected high-profile personalities and celebrities. The list includes prime ministers, presidents, a vice president, royalties, and several high-ranking government officials and politicians such as members of parliament and cabinet ministers. The same was true for bishops and archbishops and other prominent church leaders. At least one president, Pierre Nkurunziza of Burundi, who ignored the severity of the threat at his own risk, reportedly succumbed to COVID-19 barely a week after declaring that "God has cleared [coronavirus]

---

[17] Video Message of His Holiness Pope Francis on the Occasion of the Pentecost Vigil Promoted by Charis.

from Burundi's skies."[18] Concretely, the pandemic has shown how intimately humanity's fate and vulnerabilities are interconnected. For the sake of a memory that serves the future and engenders hope, it is fair to expect, as does Pope Francis, that the members of the privileged and powerful class who have experienced what it feels like to be sickened by COVID-19 will be "all the more aware of the presence of the poor in our midst and their need for help."[19] The stories or, better still, biographies of the poor locate them at the receiving end of multiple societal inequalities and injustices. Consequent upon this act of remembering, perhaps, those in positions of authority and political influence would make a firm commitment and resolve to repair broken health systems and infrastructure that have neglected the most vulnerable, right grotesque social inequalities, redress chronic economic injustices, eliminate health discrimination, and protect the poor from the vicissitude of a global economic arrangement weighted in favor of the rich and privileged. As Francis counsels, words are not enough. Quiet but genuine, moral, and radical witness is needed. Again, herein lies a critical imperative for authentic leadership that preferentially seeks out the weakest, the underprivileged, and the marginalized to restore their dignity, tend to their wounds, and provide for their needs, as we saw in chapters 1, 2, and 3.

To reiterate a point made above, in times past, humanity has suffered calamities of pandemics and plagues. Their histories are well documented. The coronavirus pandemic is the most recent in that tragic history of global public health crises. Yet, as Pope Francis points out insightfully, pandemics are not exclusively epidemiological events to be prevented or treated exclusively using scientific and technical know-how. Insightfully, Francis declared at the Eucharist in Casa Santa Marta on May 2, 2020, that "This pandemic is also a time of social

---

[18] "Nkurunziza Death: Burundi Court Rules to End Power Vacuum," *The BBC*, June 12, 2020 (www.bbc.com).

[19] "Message of Pope Francis for 2020 World Day of the Poor," 7.

crisis. A moment of crisis is a moment of choice." If COVID-19 doubles as a socioeconomic and political crisis, it is not the only one. There are other pandemics that manifest pathologies of structurally and systemically flawed socioeconomic and political models and practices. In this man-made reservoir of deadly pandemics one finds hunger, war, poverty, corruption, forced displacement, wealth inequality, ecological degradation, and the globalization of indifference. To this list we should add xenophobia, homophobia, clergy sexual abuse, and gender-based violence. By comparison, these social, economic, and political pathogens are no less transmissible and virulent in terms of their toll on human lives. They are further proof of a broken leadership. Although I refer to them here as "viruses" metaphorically, functionally they do not exist independently of society's unjust structures of discrimination, marginalization, and exclusion. Viruses do not discriminate, marginalize, or exclude people and communities, but society does.

In light of the foregoing and as a complement to economic and political plans, strategies, and solutions deployed to deal with social inequities, Pope Francis applies an epidemiological analogy: he proposes "antibodies" of a different kind to combat and overcome the menace of these social, economic, and political viruses. Ordinarily antibodies defend the body against an antigen, that is, a virus or a bacterium. They provide the bulwark of resistance to fend off the attacks of foreign substances in the body. From the perspective of the ethics of justice, equity, human rights, and human dignity, Francis prescribes a complementary and effective remedy for social pandemics in the form of "antibodies of solidarity."[20] These kinds of antibodies double as antidotes to indifference, marginalization, exclusion, and isolation. In other words, they prioritize proactive initiatives that eliminate conditions, factors, and situations that render the weakest members of society susceptible to the worst outcomes of epidemiological and social

---

[20] Pope Francis, "*Un plan para resucitar*" (A Plan to Resurrect).

pandemics. Antibodies of solidarity build a global resilience to the menace of social pandemics. I would add that "antibodies" of good leadership are also needed in a crisis. Just as it is critical to lead in a crisis, so it is crucial to lead out of a crisis. In either case, as the pandemic clearly demonstrates, scientific knowledge and technical expertise are not enough. Leadership of the kind exemplified by Pope Francis is vital in order to harness the reservoir of resources and to act decisively and compassionately in the interest of the common good.

Current and future histories of this crisis would be biased, incomplete, and contrived if we turned our backs on the suffering of so many people and on their experience of pain. It is a valid question to ask whether the concentration of solidarity, compassion, care, resilience, mutual aid, and generosity witnessed globally will vanish once the coronavirus is vanquished. For Francis, the answer lies in making a choice in favor of finding and fortifying lasting antibodies of solidarity. This quest presents a noble and worthwhile task for the time after COVID-19. Moreover, in the wake of the coronavirus pandemic, one of the greatest tragedies would be the absolutization and institutionalization of social distancing that further deepens the isolation and exclusion of poor and vulnerable people. In Pope Francis's plan, to create a future of equity and justice, it would be imperative for the global community to avoid reinforcing existing fault lines of inequalities. Besides, as many public health experts have warned, a virus knows no boundaries. It is in the interest of the international community to include all populations in measures to control and defeat the coronavirus and other global pandemics. Only an inclusive approach can guarantee effective protection for all. Essentially, according to Francis, from an ethical perspective of mutual accountability, the coronavirus crisis confronts the global community with a simple question demanding an honest answer: Where is your sister? Where is your brother? (Gn 4:9). Hence, at all levels of society, the pope emphasizes the crucial necessity for the international community to commit unreservedly to the promotion, prioritization, and practice of "the necessary antibodies of justice, charity, and solidarity," and to embrace "the alternative civilization of love" and a "civilization of hope" in which no one is left behind.[21]

In sum, as an interconnected human family, Pope Francis invites all people of goodwill to envision and labor for the emergence of a radically transformed world, one in which all assume a shared responsibility for the common good and the well-being of all. As Francis told doctors and nurses from the Lombardy region, "It's illusory to make individualism the guiding principle of society."[22] And, as we saw in chapter 5, his vision is of a new world that invests in and prioritizes the building of connections, relationships, and bridges over the construction of borders, fences, and walls. It is an imagination inspired by the behavior and attitudes of compassion and hope in the midst of pain and despair that Jesus models in the gospel. In the final analysis, for Francis, the coronavirus crisis poses a severe threat to life. Indeed, it is *primarily* a crisis of life. Consequently, the postpandemic world should be about prioritizing and valuing human life and effecting a sea change of socioeconomic and political arrangements to serve and protect human life. World leaders owe this to people who have lived and died with COVID-19. Following the logic of Francis, the ethical imperative to imbue and fortify social, economic, and political systems with antibodies of justice, charity, and solidarity ought to be the priority and task of conscientious, compassionate, courageous, and committed leaders. A few good women and men would suffice.

In what concerns the future of the mission and ministry of the church, the coronavirus pandemic renders predictions tenuous. The future holds many possibilities. No less than

---

[21] Ibid.

[22] "Pope Thanks Italian Doctors and Health Care Workers for Heroic Service during Pandemic," *Vatican News*, June 20, 2020 (www.vaticannews. va).

two-thirds of the world's population experienced isolation in involuntary huddles in order to take shelter from the violent rage of the coronavirus. This had a direct impact on congregational worship and sacramental celebration. Such developments ought not to be easily forgotten. Without underestimating its scale and cost, the task of identifying the opportunities and learning the relevant lessons of the coronavirus crisis for Christianity and the church seems a pertinent and useful exercise long after the pandemic has passed and its violent rage abated. Stephen Bullivant rightly points out that the crisis has revived the relevance and meaning of the notion of "domestic church."[23] A collaborative and broad-based process of analyzing, discerning, and rethinking the theology and mission of Christianity and the world church in all their dimensions, including sacraments, ministry, and governance, will determine whether this crisis portends a new beginning or the beginning of the end—the harbinger of a local and global ecclesial renewal or the closing chapter in the history of Christianity and the church. Absent any predictions, I dream of a post-coronavirus church with doors open to a new Pentecost that blows social distances away and frees consciences of bureaucratic, clericalist, and hierarchical structures and certainties in which believers were schooled to place their trust. I dream of a church receptive to new ways of practicing solidarity, mercy, and compassion in response to Jesus's commission to be women and men for others. In other words, people who, like Pope Francis, exercise a ministry of consolation and a preference of love for the poor, vulnerable, and underprivileged. If realized, this dream would embody Francis's model of church-as-field-hospital, where all who minister in the name of the gospel take a leaf from the book of heroic health care and frontline workers during COVID-19, and venture into existential peripheries to welcome and tend to the casualties of social, economic, political, and ecological oppression, isolation, and

---

[23] Bullivant, *Catholicism in the Time of Coronavirus,* 54–55.

exclusion. Essentially, this means a church that speaks Ubuntu: I am because you are. This represents a monumental task for the mission of the church in a postpandemic world. Pope Francis proclaimed this same message on World Mission Day 2020:

> Understanding what God is saying to us at this time of pandemic also represents a challenge for the Church's mission. Illness, suffering, fear, and isolation challenge us. The poverty of those who die alone, the abandoned, those who have lost their jobs and income, the homeless, and those who lack food challenge us. Being forced to observe social distancing and to stay at home invites us to rediscover that we need social relationships as well as our communal relationship with God. Far from increasing mistrust and indifference, this situation should make us even more attentive to our way of relating to others.

To fail to birth this kind of ecclesial reality by taking advantage of all the opportunities on offer, including the digital tools for proclaiming the Good News, would amount to a regression to a prepandemic cave devoid of the life-transforming light of the Risen Christ.

I harbor no pretension about the scope of this book. It does not exhaust the task of examining the coronavirus crisis and distilling all of its lessons for church and for *Urbi et Orbi* (To the City and to the World). This book considers one aspect of this task, that is, the requisite kind and role of leadership, and it opens a conversation. More work needs to be done, especially from the perspective of theological ethics.

At the beginning of this book, I noted that I was an admirer of Pope Francis. Looking back over the chapters, that was perhaps an understatement. Considering other aspects of the man that had escaped my awareness previously and that I have only come to appreciate more fully in the course of writing this book, a more honest admission would be to say that I am a "Franciscophile." I hold firmly the conviction that Francis is one of a very uncommon group of leaders to whom Jesus's approbation could rightly and accurately be applied: a believer, pastor, and leader in whom there is no guile (Jn 1:47). If this book reads like an account of past events, that is only because of the nature of its historical setting, namely, a particular time during the coronavirus pandemic. The protagonist is Pope Francis. The narrative style is a deliberate choice. What I present or is perceived in this book as a story from the past would be more appropriately read and appreciated as a narrative of Francis's prophetic way of life, his pastoral style of ministry, and his lifelong commitment to the things that matter for humanity.

In the final analysis, the pope is not exceptional. History is replete with accounts of heroic deeds of women and men—not all of them celebrated or immortalized—in the time of crises. A crisis is not a condition *sine qua non* for being a consoler, giving preference to the poor, celebrating the goodness in other people, adopting the resources of faith to foster hope, reaching out to people outside of one's preferred ambit, or striving for change and conversion in one's life journey. We do not need a contagious and lethal virus to make the various points contained in this book about the preferences and priorities of the pope, although they are useful for pedagogical purposes. Because, in reality, what we see and celebrate in Pope Francis's leadership style manifests as everyday gestures of faith, hope, and charity woven into his gospel-inspired ministry and expressed in genuine acts of mercy, compassion, solidarity, and tenderness.

In other words, for Francis, faith, hope, and charity follow an integrated trajectory. So do word and witness. What you see is what you get. He is neither an impressionist nor an exhibitionist, much less an opportunist. Francis does not know that he is in this script, since this book is not the outcome of an interview or biographical project. In seasons of crisis or seasons of joy, his words and deeds remain genuine manifestations of his way of life, marked by a proclivity for speaking with boldness and listening with humility. Only the consistency of faith, profundity of hope, and magnanimity of charity demonstrated by Francis and documented in the preceding chapters, possess the capacity to inspire this new imagination of what is possible. There is no shortcut. There is no alternative. Moreover, true leadership is a higher calling available to all women and men. Like every vocation in life, ongoing probation, change, and conversion are integral to the process of growth and progress. I have no doubt that Pope Francis understands that it is a long road to resurrection. If a sequel to this book were to be written, I believe that it would hardly deviate from the key aspects outlined in this book about how Francis leads, and the lessons for others in leadership in the church and the rest of the world—be it in a time of crisis or in any other time.

Suggested Readings

Faggioli, Massimo. *The Liminal Papacy of Pope Francis: Moving toward Global Catholicity* (Maryknoll, NY: Orbis Books, 2020).

Ilo, Stan Chu. *A Poor and Merciful Church: The Illuminative Ecclesiology of Pope Francis* (Maryknoll, NY: Orbis Books, 2018).

Ivereigh, Austen. *Wounded Shepherd: Pope Francis's Struggle to Convert the Catholic Church* (New York: Henry Holt, 2020).

Lamb, Christopher. *The Outsider: Pope Francis and His Battle to Reform the Church* (Maryknoll, NY: Orbis Books, 2020).

Lowney, Chris. *Pope Francis: Why He Leads the Way He Leads: Lessons from the First Jesuit Pope* (Chicago: Loyola Press, 2013).

McElwee, Joshua J., and Cindy Wooden, eds. *A Pope Francis Lexicon* (Collegeville, MN: Liturgical Press, 2018).

O'Connell, Gerard. *The Election of Pope Francis: An Inside Account of the Conclave That Changed History* (Maryknoll, NY: Orbis Books, 2019).

Wall, Barbara, and Massimo Faggioli, eds. *Pope Francis: A Voice for Mercy, Justice, Love, and Care for the Earth* (Maryknoll, NY: Orbis Books, 2019).

Index